Investing with Anthony Bolton

Investing with Anthony Bolton

The anatomy of a stock market phenomenon

By Jonathan Davis

Published by Harriman House Ltd
in association with
Investor Publishing Ltd

HARRIMAN HOUSE LTD

43 Chapel Street
Petersfield
Hampshire
GU32 3DY
GREAT BRITAIN

Tel: +44 (0)1730 233870
Fax: +44 (0)1730 233880
Email: enquiries@harriman-house.com
Website: www.harriman-house.com

First published in Great Britain in 2004
Copyright: Investor Publishing 2004 except
Chapter 2 Anthony Bolton 2004

Published by Harriman House Ltd
In association with Investor Publishing Ltd
37 Great Pulteney Street, Bath, BA2 4DA
Tel: +44 (0)1225 442508
Fax: +44 (0) 1225 444973
Website: www.intelligent-investor.co.uk

The right of Jonathan Davis to be identified as the author has been asserted
in accordance with the Copyright, Design and Patents Act 1988.

ISBN 1-897-59750-9

British Library Cataloguing in Publication Data
A CIP catalogue record for this book can be obtained from the British Library.

Printed and bound by Biddles Ltd, Kings Lynn, Norfolk.

Contents

About the author

Jonathan Davis has been writing about financial markets and the City for 25 years. After graduating from Cambridge University his early career was spent as a business journalist on national newspapers, the *Sunday Telegraph*, *The Times* and *The Economist*. Since 1991, after a year on the Sloan Fellowship programme at MIT's Sloan School of Management, he has run his own specialist publishing and consultancy business. He

has been writing a popular column about investment in *The Independent* since 1995. His books include *Money Makers*, a study of successful professional investors, and a primer on bridge. He is chairman of Investor Publishing, which specialises in publishing high quality material on money and investment, and the founding editor of the specialist newsletter *Intelligent Investor*. For more information, visit www.intelligent-investor.co.uk.

What they say about Anthony Bolton

Neil Woodford, Head of Investment, Invesco Perpetual

"Anthony Bolton is an exceptional investor. His focus on producing excellent long-term performance has never been swayed by fashion or market pressures and he has maintained his investment integrity throughout varying market conditions. These are the disciplines that quality fund managers exhibit."

John Armitage, Director, Egerton Capital

"Anthony Bolton's professional achievement has been combined with great modesty. He has all the good attributes of success and none of the bad. Many people underestimate what it takes to be as successful as he has been."

Jeff Prestridge, Personal Finance Editor, Mail on Sunday

"In an industry where fund manager loyalty is sadly lacking, Anthony Bolton is living proof that loyalty can pay handsomely, not only for employers but more importantly for investors. For the past 25 years, he has run the good ship Fidelity Special Situations like a master commander. His investment record is exemplary and living proof that long term investment in equities can really pay."

Patrick Collinson, Personal Finance Editor, The Guardian

"Anthony Bolton's name adds enormous weight and gravitas to any article on investment. Over the years he has become perhaps the most respected and powerful fund manager in the country. In other individuals, such power would make them fearsomely self-important, yet Anthony Bolton has always remained accessible to the press and investors. He's alert to the fact that behind it all, he's running money on behalf of tens of thousands of small investors, and it's their interests, rather than his ego, that count above all."

Nigel Thomas, UK equity fund manager at Framlington

"Anthony Bolton's intellect and agile mind make him the very best in our industry. His ability to manage a large fund, with such foresight, is without peer in the UK stockmarket."

Introduction

Anthony Bolton in the office overlooking St Paul's Cathedral

Introduction

There are very few professional investors of whom it can truly be said: "this is one of the greats". Scan the pages of the newspapers and the specialist investment magazines, where promises of exceptional performance are liberally distributed, in editorial and advertising alike, and you might all too easily form a different impression. Fund management remains a competitive, sales-driven business: "25% performance and 75% marketing", as the legendary Warren Buffett once drily observed.

Hundreds of academic studies over the past thirty years have underlined what many investors have learnt for themselves through experience: that it is remarkably difficult even for highly talented fund managers to beat the market consistently over any length of time. That is one reason why so-called 'passive investing', in which investors buy funds that mechanically track the performance of the major market indices, has grown to become such a significant part of the modern investment game.

Yet exceptional talents who have shown they can outperform their benchmark indices on a consistent basis over many years do exist. They are rightly able to command a hefty premium for their services, as well as attention from headhunters and the respect of their peers. Some of the best and brightest go off these days to join hedge funds, the current investment fad (not always with spectacular results). Others opt to set up their own investment companies where they can pursue their craft without the pressures that working in a large corporate environment usually brings.

In the field of unit trusts, the staple diet of millions of private investors, it is rare for the best fund managers to avoid these tempting alternatives and stay the course of an entire career. Of those who have done just that, one man by common consent stands head and shoulders above nearly all the rest for the consistency and integrity of his performance. In polls of professional investors, he is the fund manager most regularly rated the one his peers admire most. The flagship fund he runs for Fidelity International has the best record of any unit trust over the past 25 years: a record indeed that is twice as good over the period as that of the next best surviving UK equity fund.

That man is Anthony Bolton, the subject of this book. In December 2004 Bolton celebrates the 25th anniversary of the launch of his UK equity fund, Fidelity Special Situations. If you had been lucky or smart enough to invest £1,000 in the fund at launch, you would today have more than eighty times that initial investment. Your initial investment would today (as at December 2004) be worth £90,000, some four times what you would have if you had simply tracked the UK stock market over the same period (which, it should be remembered, has itself been one of the greatest times in modern history to own shares).

The fund's performance translates to a compound rate of return of nearly 20% per annum, sustained over a quarter of a century – a phenomenal record that stands comparison with the biggest names in American fund management. Even more remarkable is the fact that his performance has remained so consistently strong over the whole period, despite a thousandfold increase in the size of the fund. No other professional working in Bolton's field can match this record of enduring success.

The obvious question that arises then is: how has he done it? This book, timed to coincide with the 25th anniversary of the fund's launch, attempts to look more closely at the things that have contributed to its success. It falls into four distinct sections:

- The first chapter is a profile of Anthony Bolton and his funds. It builds on and updates the account of his methods that formed part of my book Money Makers (1998). Researching my newspaper columns, newsletter and books has given me the opportunity to hold many conversations with Bolton since. It has also enabled me to meet and study scores of other professional investors. While I am not known as a great fan of active managers in general, he is unquestionably one of a very small number who deserve the title of 'star'.

- In the second chapter, Anthony Bolton gives his own account of his time at the helm of Fidelity Special Situations – how it all began, the methods he uses to achieve his results, and the lessons he has learnt from 25 years mastering the craft of professional investment. Although he has been the subject of numerous short profiles in the past, this is the first time that he has set out his own account of the fund and his philosophy of investment at length.

HOW THE FUND HAS GROWN
The value of £1,000 invested at launch

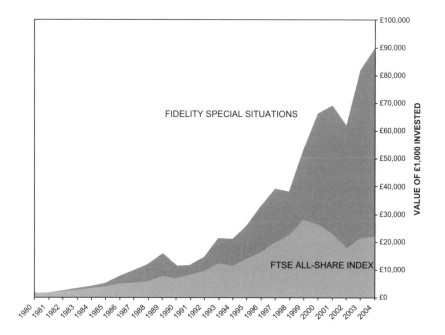

- The third chapter takes an in-depth look at the performance of the Fidelity Special Situation fund over the course of its 25-year history and asks the question: how good and how consistent has it really been? Interpreting fund performance statistics can be a hazardous business, and notoriously full of pitfalls for the unwary. As well as providing detailed performance numbers, the chapter draws on assessments by well-regarded independent fund analysts.

- The concluding chapter assesses the contribution that Anthony has made in his years of running money, and speculates on the reasons for his and Fidelity's exceptional success. As one of the first fund managers to be recruited when Fidelity set up their operation in Europe in 1979, he has been an influential figure in the successful development of their business. The section finishes with some broader observations about the lessons that investors might draw from a study of the Anthony Bolton phenomenon.

In the Appendices, the reader will find more data on the performance of Fidelity Special Situations, detailed assessments of the fund's style and risk profile by professional fund analysts, and extracts from an early fund report and a detailed example of a typical piece of Fidelity corporate analysis. This supplementary material is designed to fill out the picture of how Bolton goes about his business.

* * * * * * *

One of America's most respected investment consultants, Charlie Ellis, told me some years ago that he had come to the conclusion after many years of experience that integrity, rather than performance, was the most important quality of all to look for when seeking a professional investment adviser or firm. "Performance is obviously important, but what you need most as an investor", says Charlie, "is confidence that your investment manager is actively, relentlessly putting your interests first, year in year out".

It has been an agreeable task to undertake a project that analyses the achievements of one fund manager whose integrity has never been in question, and who has rarely disappointed the faith of those who have put their money into his care. The fact that he is one of the nicest men you are likely to meet has little to do with Anthony Bolton's success – the City rewards the ruthless and the unpleasant just as readily as the charming and well-mannered – but it certainly makes chronicling the fact far more pleasurable.

Jonathan Davis
Chairman, Investor Publishing
Author, columnist and publisher

1

The professional's professional

The man and his funds

Second to none

When European finance directors are surveyed to find out which investment management firms are the most highly regarded in their sphere, one name repeatedly appears at or near the top. That firm is Fidelity International, an affiliate of the Boston-based American firm. Fidelity launched its first UK unit trust in 1979, since when it has grown to become one of the largest and most successful independent fund management companies in Europe. Anthony Bolton is their *galactico*, the star performer whose investment expertise and success has come to define the firm and its success on this side of the Atlantic. If anyone merits the title of the 'professional's professional' in the UK investment scene, this is the man. Quiet and thoughtful, and anything but flash, Bolton is a model of what the modern professional investment manager should be: clear-sighted, disciplined, hardworking and conscientious, with a track record of consistent outperformance in all his funds.

It is unwise to use the term 'technocrat' in the context of anything so volatile and variable as the stock market. As all financial markets essentially deal in uncertainty, the business of investment can never be reduced to a science. But Bolton has done as much as anyone in the UK to demonstrate that the best principles of engineering, the subject he studied at university, can be profitably applied to the art of picking stocks. The paradox is that he has done it by investing in the kind of shares that most others won't touch with a bargepole. He is a contrarian investor, someone who takes positive delight in scouring the orphan areas of the stock market, looking for shares that are damaged or unloved, but capable of redemption. The strategy has its risks, even for a diversified fund, but it has worked like a dream over the 25 years that his funds have been on the market, and that is what ultimately counts for any professional fund manager.

So successful have his methods been that Bolton now manages more than £4 billion of other people's money in one fund alone, Fidelity Special Situations. Some 250,000 people, mostly individuals, are investors in the fund, which is the best performing fund of its kind over its 25-year history. For a good part of his career, Bolton also managed a group of funds that invested in Continental Europe, with equally conspicuous success. Between 2001 and 2003, he handed over his European responsibilities to concentrate once more on his UK funds. The money he manages now is split between the Fidelity Special Situations Fund, and a sister investment trust, Fidelity Special Values. Bolton's formal title is that of a Managing Director of Fidelity Investments, but his real job is that of spearheading the firm's fund management effort.

All the funds that Bolton has managed have consistently outstanding track records. Since their launches in 1979 and 1985, his two main funds, the Special Situations and European funds, for example, have both achieved a compound annual rate of return of around 20% while under his management, comfortably beating the market and their peer group in both cases. Both also command best-of-class ratings from the leading independent fund rating services such as Standard & Poor's and Morningstar. The funds and their manager have won countless industry awards, as well as extravagant plaudits from financial advisers. (A sample: "a bloody phenomenon" – Darius McDermott at Chelsea Financial Advisers; "fantastically gifted" – James Calder of Bestinvest; "something of a genius" – Robert Lockie of Chelsea Financial Planning).[2] More importantly perhaps, in a poll of leading fund managers conducted by Sunday Business in 2003, when asked to nominate the competitor they most admired, five of the ten named Bolton.[3]

Some of this, in a business that is as notoriously marketing-led as fund management, can be written off as flam and/or hyperbole. Yet there is real substance behind the gloss. It is not a surprise to see serious observers describe Bolton in print as Britain's answer to Peter Lynch, a legendary Irish-American stockpicker who for thirteen years ran the world's largest mutual fund, the Magellan fund, for Fidelity in the United States. The comparison with Lynch, whose style can best be described as hyperactive, is hardly an exact one, but the fact that it can be made at all shows the measure of Bolton's standing in the professional investment community. Lynch is one of the genuine modern masters of the investment game; and if there is an equivalent to be found in the UK, Bolton is, in the view of many cognoscenti, the nearest thing that we have to such a phenomenon.

---

[1] Figures as at 31st August 2004.

[2] Quoted in Bloomberg Money August 2004

[3] It is an indication of the way that Bolton works that three of the five who nominated him said that they had never met him.

Anthony Bolton at work September 2004

An orderly mind

To meet, Bolton is a slim, unobtrusive figure with bright eyes and slightly curly, now greying hair. He speaks quietly but clearly, and mostly in complete sentences, the telltale sign of an orderly mind. He gives off an image of cool and quiet efficiency, is unfailingly courteous in company, and would certainly not look out of place in a serious university. You gain the impression that there is little he does with his life that is not deliberate. But that, intriguingly, proves not to be entirely the case. This is someone who had to be kicked out of bed by his father to get a job on leaving university, and who drifted into the City by chance rather than from any lifelong conviction that he was destined to make money from buying and selling shares. This leisurely start to life has not stopped him becoming one of the most highly sought after fund managers in a highly competitive, well renumerated business whose top performers can earn millions in a single year.

To find Bolton's office, you have to take a trip to the heart of the City, to a large modern office block that overlooks St Paul's Cathedral. The site formerly housed a large American bank whose global ambitions proved to be greater than its capabilities. It is unquestionably Fidelity's grandest office yet, with a marbled entrance hall and a selection of David Hockney prints on the walls, reflecting the success of the firm's foray into Europe. Bolton's office is located on the second floor, where he sits at a standard issue desk, facing away from the view of Sir Christopher Wren's glorious creation outside. On a shelf behind his desk is a row of books that contain, in date order, his notes on all the meetings with companies that he has recorded and kept over the years. (There are over sixty in all, of which more than 80% concern his meetings with UK companies.) There is a computer screen in the corner, and on the walls family photographs and some of the numerous industry awards his efforts have won over the years. The overall impression is strongly reminiscent of a university professor's office. This is orderly, functional space, and not much more. There is little to indicate that this is where arguably the best money manager the UK has produced goes about his business.

By his own admission, and that of his admirers, Bolton's great strength as an investor is that he is an emotionally placid individual, who is capable of taking setbacks with fortitude. "You have to be a fairly calm person to be a fund manager" is his own admission. "The great thing about him," says Peter Jeffreys, a former colleague who went on from Fidelity to co-found the ratings firm Fund Research, "is that everything he does is completely straight up and down. There is absolutely no side to him, none at all." Sir Charles Fraser, a fund director, asked to provide an anecdote about Bolton, replied simply: "I have none. He is not an anecdote sort of person." Less immediately obvious is the high degree of commitment and organisation that Bolton brings to his task. Like the majority of successful professional investment managers, he believes that to be a professional investor, you have to be wholly absorbed by the markets. "I think you have got to be fanatical about it", he says, "because investing is continuous and intangible. There's no beginning or end to it, and there is always something new that needs delving into. I think you have to be completely taken by it to do well. If I look at the investment managers I admire, none of them do it part time."[4]

---

[4] Unless specifically attributed to another source, all the direct quotations in this section are from interviews with the author.

He concedes that it may be different for those, such as George Soros, the hedge fund speculator, who specialise in making big bets on the macroeconomic outlook. For those two or three decisions a year, assuming they are the right ones, and they are backed heavily, can be all the difference between success and failure. But for investors who specialise in picking stocks, as Bolton does, there is no alternative to being fanatical. When he started, he had only 20-30 shares to look after. But now, thanks to the success of his funds, which have grown a hundredfold in size since 1987, there are nearly two hundred stocks to track in his various portfolios. It requires not just hard work, but the support of a large team of analysts to keep tabs on what they are all doing. At the last count, there were more than 50 analysts at Fidelity in London whose work he could call upon. He has helped to train many of them himself in the art of stock analysis, Fidelity style. They know what he wants and he has faith in what they produce.

It would be impossible for an individual to sustain the quality of his performance in these circumstances without both high levels of enthusiasm and the ability to make quick decisions. Peter Lynch had exceptional energy, but even he decided to retire from running Fidelity's Magellan fund in 1990 after only thirteen years, pleading the relentless pressure of work. At the age of 54, Bolton has lasted nearly twice as long in the same arduous and stressful job. He shows no signs of tiring of the investment game, though the burden of following so many companies has prompted him to cut back on his research and travel commitments by handing over responsibility for his European funds to two colleagues. He plans to go on running his funds for a while yet, but "not forever, as it takes a lot out of you." His working week remains a long one. Given the emphasis that Fidelity places on indepth research, the amount of paperwork alone he has to shift is formidable.

Devoted to detail

A typical day for Bolton begins with him leaving home in West Sussex at 6.30 a.m. to catch a train to London. He reads the Financial Times on the train and also does his homework on one or more of the companies he will be seeing later. On the way to and from the station he catches up on the forty or so voicemails he has each day. His working week revolves around company meetings. When he was covering both UK and continental companies, it was not unknown to do as many as five or six a day, and there are many others for which a colleague will provide a report. Fidelity as a group sees an average of fifteen to twenty companies a day in London, sometimes more, either in its offices, at the companies themselves or by conference call. Few fund management companies do more to stay in contact with existing and potential investments.[5]

Each company is analysed beforehand in detail by the in-house analysts, and becomes the subject of a detailed pack of information, several pages long, covering the key financial data, plus brokers' views and any other relevant material, such as press cuttings and so on. The meetings are an opportunity for Bolton and his colleagues to ask questions of the management and keep up to date on how the business is going. All these meetings are written up afterwards, though rarely at length. Bolton himself takes his own hand-written notes, usually two or three pages long, which he files neatly away in the books behind his desk. He brings them out later to check that companies have not changed their tune since he last saw them. Browsing through them gives an insight into the austerity of his methods: in the dozen or so volumes I looked at one day, there was not a single anecdote, piece of gossip or personal remark to be found (and not even a doodle, for that matter). His *modus operandi* is one that Charles Dickens' Mr Gradgrind ("facts, facts, facts") would recognise and applaud. It requires not just brains, but intense concentration on the task in hand.

Unusually, in addition to Fidelity's own analysis and research bought in from brokers and others, Bolton also likes to look at a number of share price charts before seeing companies, in order to see what their recent price action has been. Add all this up, and you have a pile of daily paperwork that would make Sir Humphrey Appleby, the mandarin of Yes Minister, proud. Like a government minister, in some ways Bolton has become a slave to his boxes. It is one reason why he normally gets home at eight in the evening, and says he dreads the end of holidays because of the huge pile of files that he knows will be awaiting him on his return. One way he escapes from the pressure of work is by composing classical music, an activity he has recently resumed after having been very keen as a child. It leaves little time for socialising with

---

[5] "There's no great secret to investment success", Bolton told Martin Baker of the Daily Telegraph in March 2004. "You need a method and good information. I think we know our companies better than other people. Get to know the companies you invest in. That's the ultimate test."

his professional peers, or even his Fidelity colleagues. He is not by his own admission "a going out for a beer person. I commute in from the country. I don't do a lot of evening things. I like to get home."[6]

"There is an awful lot of reading", he adds, with more than a hint of weariness. "One reason I commute by train is that I can kill off quite a lot of it that way. You have to know what you are looking for because you can become mesmerised by the sheer volume of it all, and lulled into complete inactivity. I like to screen a lot of things and most of the broker material is frankly unnecessary at least for my purpose. There are certain analysts whom I rate, and I know to look out for their stuff. If the note is a sell and it's a company I don't own, I won't even look at it. If it's a sell and I do own it, then obviously I'll want to have a quick look. But you have got to weed out the dross." This requires both discipline and hard work, two qualities for which Bolton is renowned, even amongst his colleagues.[7]

The background briefing material that Fidelity analysts prepare on each company is presented in a standardised house format. Even so, the sheer weight of material means, says Bolton, that "you have to have a system to get through, otherwise you are sunk". Some of his fund manager colleagues survive by ignoring all the brokers' research, preferring to stick to in-house material alone. But this is not Bolton's style. "I don't have that approach. You never know where the next idea is going to come from." An eclectic mind, he insists, is needed to make his style of investing have any chance of working.

When companies come to visit, as they do in ever growing numbers, Bolton says it is important that they demonstrate that the managements know their business. "While some investors put a lot of emphasis on the quality of management, I'm more of a Warren Buffett follower in that I would rather have a good business run by average management than the other way round. I find that people who impress you in meetings are not necessarily the best managers." He mentions John Gunn, who was widely lauded for a while in the 1980s as the best manager in the City. A few years later, his company, British & Commonwealth, was bust.

[6] Daily Telegraph, January 10th 2004

[7] Sally Walden, who has worked alongside Bolton for more than twenty years, says that he is the most efficient manager of time that she has ever come across. It is rare for any moment of his working day to be wasted.

"I like managements who are consistent in what they say. I dislike hyperbole, managers who consistently overegg the pudding." He is more concerned to see what companies are saying about their products: "If they put great emphasis on one product when they come to see us, and next time fail to mention it at all, we will obviously start to get worried. You are obviously looking to read between the lines." If a competitor says something positive about a company's product range, it counts for twice as much as the company saying the same thing itself. (A more detailed summary of Bolton's views on what companies can do to satisfy investors can be found in the Appendix on page 160.)

A chance beginning

Given such a highly formalised approach to his work, it comes as something of a surprise to learn that Bolton only drifted into the business of investing by chance. His early experience was gained at a small and rather risqué merchant bank called Keyser Ullmann. In its heyday in the early 1970s, it enjoyed a reputation for adventurousness, later somewhat tarnished by a number of unsuccessful and controversial deals that eventually resulted in the bank disappearing as an independent entity. Bolton went there as the bank's "first and last graduate trainee". He had studied engineering at Cambridge, but says that after two years of the subject the "one thing I was pretty certain of was that I didn't want to become an engineer". When the time came to leave university in 1971, he did so without having a job lined up.

About three weeks after the end of his final summer holidays, Bolton's barrister father, who had previously encouraged him to take his time over deciding what to do, suddenly began to apply pressure on him to make a more positive attempt to find a job. A businessman friend of the family suggested he think about the City, and another family friend, a stockbroker, gave him an introduction to Keyser Ullmann, which at the time was still growing fast and had decided (according to Bolton) that "this graduate training business sounded a good idea". By such strange quirks of chance are successful careers often launched.

Unlike many other successful investors, Bolton did not set out to find a job as an investment manager, nor did he arrive in the business with any burning ambition to make money from the markets. As he points out, amongst his peer group at university, corporate finance was still very much the 'in thing' for those who went into the City. Investment management was regarded as second-division stuff. "Corporate finance had the glamour attached to it", he recalls, "and investment management was hardly known as an industry." He himself had no prior interest in the markets, and knew nothing about them. Not for him a history of trading stamps, or other moneymaking schemes, while he was a child. Unlike many of the greatest investors, whose motivation to succeed often stems from a poor background, Bolton had a conventional middle class upbringing.

Bolton spent five years at Keyser Ullmann, and reckons he got good training while he was there, despite the bank's subsequent problems. He started as a general trainee, "behind the tills, doling out the money, trooping off to the money markets, where they all went around in top hats in those days". After a brief stint in administration, he spent a little time on the investment side, and it was there that he finally "picked up the bug of stocks and shares". He was offered a job as a research assistant in the investment arm of the bank. It was here that his career as an investment manager began. The investment side was separate from the rest of the bank and most of the money it managed was in investment trusts. This meant, says Bolton, that when the bank got into difficulties and depositors started taking their money away, his side of the business remained largely unaffected.

Developing a style

Three things about the way that Keyser Ullmann managed money proved influential in the development of Bolton's style as an investor. One was that they specialised in smaller companies, something that remains one of his trademarks today. The second was that they went out and visited the companies they owned. This was rather novel at the time, when most investment managers still relied heavily on stockbrokers to bring them information and ideas. Third, one of the directors was interested in technical analysis, or the use of share price charts, to supplement conventional fundamental analysis of shares. This too remains one of Bolton's interests.

His job as an assistant to one of the fund managers included writing a few paragraphs on each company's half-yearly and annual results, saying whether or not the shares still looked reasonable investments. He remembers the fascination of discovering the Datastream machine, then something of a novelty in the City, which allowed him to search ('screen') the universe of stocks and shares looking for those which met common specified characteristics.[8] Nevertheless, he says, it took him quite a while before he fully understood how the business worked.

Bolton had to cut his teeth as an investor in the scary markets of 1973/75, when the secondary banking crisis was at its height, and the stock market endured its worst decline in living memory. He remembers lunches at which all the other fund managers spent their time boasting about how little money they actually had invested. Instead they seemed to be competing against each other to see who had most of their money in cash. "There was a feeling of: What have I got into? Is the whole world going to end? Would the stock market ever stop going down?". It did, but it was not long before Bolton had decided that, with all the problems at Keyser Ullmann, now was a good time to move on. After a few interviews, he was offered a job as a fund manager by the Schlesinger group, which was owned by a wealthy South African family with property and financial interests in London. Among them was a unit trust company, run by Richard Timberlake and Peter Baker.

Both men proved influential in the development of Bolton's career as an investor. Baker was the one with most of the investment ideas, while Timberlake, something of a pioneer in the modern fund management business, concentrated on the marketing. The former, says Bolton, had a very objective view of investment and was always willing to judge an idea on its merits. "If you could make a good case for something, he would look at it. I always felt that if the tea lady came in and said you ought to buy ICI and these are the reasons why, he would be prepared to listen."

Baker was also mathematically minded, with an interest in how to price options using mathematical models. He was one of the first people in this country to take an interest in the quantitative techniques associated with modern portfolio theory. Noting how academic research had demonstrated the difficulty of beating the market averages, he also launched an index-tracking fund, a concept that in those days was well ahead of its time. During this period Bolton had a hand in running seven or eight different funds,

---

[8] Datastream is an information service whose extensive database allows the user to trawl through a huge raft of historical information, including share prices, bond prices, economic data and company results. Thanks to the internet and improved telecommunications, allowing fast data transfer, such information is now virtually a commodity for any professional working in the City or the West End.

doing "a bit of everything". One of these funds was a 'special situations' fund, a type with which Bolton has been closely associated ever since.

Schlesingers was not all that stable an environment however. There were constant rumours that it was for sale. South Africans, says Bolton, are "very much dealers, they like to buy and sell things, not to hang on to them". So when the second of his bosses, Richard Timberlake, was recruited by Fidelity to help set up a UK operation for the first time in 1979, Bolton let him know that he was interested in following him there. At the time, he says, he did not even know who Fidelity were. When he discovered that they were the biggest independent investment management firm in the United States, with a reputation for consistent performance, based on in-depth fundamental analysis, it clearly helped. As a result, he became one of the first two investment managers that Fidelity International recruited. He was 29, with only limited experience but the great advantage of being known to the new managing director.

While from today's perspective opting to join Fidelity may seem like an obvious career move, that was not the way it appeared to many at the time. The Department of Trade, says Timberlake, had never authorised a foreign group to run retail funds in the UK before, and insisted on several conditions before allowing Fidelity even to set up its stall. Big Bang, the act of deregulation which was to sweep away many of the cosy closed shops that had long prevailed in the Square Mile, was still seven years in the future. Exchange controls had only been lifted a few months before and business sentiment remained fragile. Inflation was out of control. The pro-capitalist government of Margaret Thatcher was still very much feeling its way after the Conservative Party's election victory earlier in the year.

Few in the City had heard of Fidelity, and those who had were often not impressed by the workaholic methods of American business. "My brother worked for Fidelity's auditors and I was told all sorts of horrific things about hiring and firing and what Americans were like", recalls Timberlake. Bill Byrnes, the Fidelity man charged with overseeing the launch of its UK operations, says; "We were a fledgling investment management company struggling to establish itself in the United Kingdom, operating in a recessionary period of soaring inflation, sky-high interest rates and wobbly equity markets. To top it off, Fidelity International had an association with an American company at a time when American invaders were viewed (not entirely unfairly) as short-term

Bill Byrnes (left) and Richard Timberlake: recruited Anthony Bolton to Fidelity

opportunists who fled the scene at the first indication of adverse circumstances."
It therefore took some courage to join this unknown ship.

Starting out at Fidelity

Timberlake asked Bolton to run a special situations fund, as this was the one
that he had most enjoyed when he was at Schlesingers, though it was not top
of Fidelity's priorities in the early years. (Byrnes and Timberlake in fact tried to
persuade their new recruit to run a Japanese fund for them, an invitation that
was politely refused.) Ironically, in view of what was to happen later, Special
Situations proved the hardest of Fidelity's original funds to sell. According to
Barry Bateman, who joined the firm on the marketing side in 1981, the fund
struggled along at around £2-£3 million in size for quite some time. "One
reason I think" says Bateman, who is now Vice Chairman of Fidelity
International and responsible for all of Fidelity's non-American businesses, "is
that people saw us as an international fund manager and so at first they
naturally thought of using us for international, rather than for UK funds. It was
quite some time before we built up a track record and people began to commit
to Special Situations". At one stage, the sales team were even offered double
commission to help get sales moving. It was only in the second half of the
1980s, when the fund appeared at the top of the five-year performance tables
for the first time, that investors began to buy the fund in substantial volumes.

What, exactly, is a special situations fund? At one level, the answer is obvious. It is a fund that looks to invest in companies which are facing unusual and exceptional circumstances, and where any turnaround in fortunes can be anticipated to produce a profit within a relatively short time. "Almost any share at a particular time can be a special situation", is how Bolton described it in his first manager's report on the new fund. "In general it will be a company attractively valued in relation to net assets, dividend yield or future earnings per share, but additionally having some other specific attraction that could have a positive short term influence on the share price." This might be a takeover, a new issue, a change of management, a recapitalisation or some other triggering event – over the years, as we shall see, Bolton has refined and analysed what he does in some detail.

But at the time he started his Fidelity fund, one of its greatest advantages, he admits now, was precisely the fact that hardly anybody was actually quite sure what the term meant. There was, he recalls, a general perception that it was an 'aggressive' (i.e. risk-seeking) fund which looked for capital growth opportunities outside the ranks of the blue chips. Tipping potential takeover candidates was one of the routes that investors found relatively easy to grasp. The initial reports emphasised that Bolton was looking for quick profits, and willing to live with above average volatility. But beyond that, there was – and remains – plenty of scope to experiment. The flexibility of the 'special situations' concept has given Bolton the leeway over the years to develop his own distinctive style of investment. It is the kind of fund that appeals to those who believe that investment managers with exceptional talent can make a big difference, whatever the academics may say about the difficulty of finding a manager who can beat the market consistently over time.

The association with Fidelity has clearly worked out well for both parties. It is difficult for anyone unfamiliar with the American investment scene to conceive of the huge influence that Fidelity enjoys in the United States. It is not only the world's largest independent investment management company, but has long been prominent in helping to shape the way that both the marketing of the investment business and professional standards in investment management have developed since World War II. Fidelity was one of the first firms to invest heavily in fundamental research, one of the first to see the need for recruiting and training the best brains to a business previously regarded as something of a backwater in the financial industry, and also one of the first to pioneer the direct marketing of collective investment vehicles to ordinary investors.

The great bull market of the 1980s and 1990s has put vast amounts of money in its hands. The rapid growth has created adjustment problems from time to time, but the company rolled on like a juggernaut through the bear market of 2000-2003. In 2004, Fidelity Management and Research, the Boston company, was running over 180 different funds and had more than $1 trillion in funds under its management. This, to put it in some context, is more than the total amount of pension fund money that the five largest pension fund managers in the UK run between them. It is equivalent to around 40% of the entire capitalisation of the London stock market. So large and influential has the firm become that the US now boasts newsletters that do nothing but monitor what is happening to Fidelity's army of funds. Its international affiliate, Fidelity International, of which the UK office is a part, has also grown steadily with more than $180 billion in assets under management. Its fund range today includes more than 30 UK retail funds and more than 250 offshore funds.

Despite its many years of growth, the original Fidelity business in Boston remains a private company controlled by the Johnson family, which started it in 1946, and other senior management. (Fidelity International however, is run as an independent business.) Ned Johnson is the second generation of the family to preside over its operations and, unusually for such family dynasties, his tenure has been every bit as successful as that of his father, a charismatic figure known to everyone inside and outside the industry simply as 'Mister Johnson'.[9] Unusually also, for a family firm in the fund business, the investment methods favoured by father and son are rather different. Whereas Mister Johnson liked to give individual fund managers their heads to invest in whatever personal style suited them, however idiosyncratic, his son has shaped the modern firm around a belief in the overriding importance of research, both fundamental and technical. (Individual fund managers are still encouraged to back their own judgements. The way that the Magellan fund is run, for example, has been very different since Peter Lynch retired in 1990.) He also takes a ruthlessly utilitarian approach to his employees. While Fidelity's fund managers are paid handsomely, and enjoy high quality technical support, those who fail to deliver sustained performance are ultimately shown the door.

---

[9] Ned Johnson's daughter Abigail is now President of Fidelity Management and Research.

Peter Lynch, Fidelity's most famous US fund manager

This highly competitive environment does not suit every kind of fund manager, but those who like it tend to like it a lot and prosper, as Bolton has done. A key feature of the Fidelity approach is that the fund managers are left to get on with running their funds, largely unhindered by other responsibilities. The running of the fund management team and investment process is left to the chief investment officer, while more recently, in response to the growing emphasis placed on corporate governance, another director handles the routine (though sometimes delicate) business of managing relationships with the companies in which the firm's funds own shares. The marketing and administration of the business is run from a separate office outside London. Whereas at many investment banks, a spell in investment management is seen merely as a stepping stone on the ladder to the top of the bank, at Fidelity fund management is the end itself.

"The Peter Lynch mould at Fidelity", says Bolton, "is that you've got to let the investment people spend all their time running their investments. If you mix in other things as well, the investment is likely to suffer." The round of daily meetings with companies leaves little time for anything else. It is an article of faith that the Fidelity way is the best. Rather than recruiting from outside, virtually all the firm's portfolio managers, and a number of its analysts, are trained from scratch in-house to ensure consistency in the firm's investment approach. Again it may not be everyone's cup of tea, but for those who enjoy the discipline of being part of a tightly managed family, it works. The recruitment process is undoubtedly helped by the power of the Fidelity brand. In a survey of 500 investment professionals reported by the Financial Times in 2003, Fidelity topped the list of most highly regarded fund managers for the fourth year in a row.

One simple insight

Bolton started managing his Special Situations fund in 1979. In 1985 he took on the management of Fidelity's first European fund as well, and ran it and its sister investment trust until 2001, when he began the handover to a colleague, Tim McCarron.[10] For a number of years he also managed an offshore European fund based in Luxembourg. At one point Bolton had overall responsibility for some £10 billion of other people's money, a prodigious sum for one individual to manage. His two pools of money – Europe and UK Special Situations – are properly judged in isolation, but there are some common underlying principles that have governed the way he has managed all the money entrusted to him. Most of these principles can be clearly traced back to the ideas that Bolton identified as having force in his very early years at Keyser Ullmann and Schlesingers.

The big insight that Bolton has carried with him throughout his career can be quickly summarised. It is simply this: that you have to do something different from everyone else in order to achieve better results. Or in his words: "If you want to outperform other people, you have got to hold something different from other people. If you want to outperform the market, as everyone expects you to do, the one thing you mustn't hold is the market itself. You certainly

---

[10] McCarron took responsibility for the investment trust first, and after that went well took on the unit trust as well, completing the transition in January 2003. Another Fidelity fund manager, Graham Clapp, took on the offshore European fund at that point.

shouldn't hold the market and do lots of dealing as well, because the transaction costs will punish you. You have got to be different." In his case, this has pushed him first in the direction of small, rather than large, quoted companies; and then towards companies which for a variety of reasons are unloved and unfashionable, but where it is possible to foresee a positive change in the near to medium-term future.

"I manage my funds with an above average risk profile, based on contrarian type stocks", is how he sums up his approach. "My ideal is a company where things have gone wrong, but where it looks as if things may be changing. I am looking for stocks that are unfashionable and cheap, but where there is something which will recapture investors' attention before too long." The idea of looking at shares which are out of favour is not of course new. In the UK, it is almost seventy years since M&G, the pioneer of the unit trust industry, launched its first Recovery Fund. That was based on the idea that you could do well out of buying shares in companies which were recovering from recession or some other setback, either external or self-inflicted. Conventional recovery stocks of this type have always been a big component of Bolton's special situation portfolios, and indeed have become more prominent in the last few years.

But they are not the only types of special situation he looks for. He also looks for companies which are under-researched, and which are therefore unlikely to be properly valued, and for companies that have growth potential that nobody else has yet recognised. In fact, Bolton's main achievement is to have taken his basic concept of being different from the pack and pushed it further than M&G, or any other mainstream fund management company, has so far dared to take it. There is a price to be paid for this in terms of risk. Although he has always insisted on a well-diversified fund, it means he has found himself holding a lot of stocks that most people would think twice about owning. That doesn't always play well with the armies of consultants who these days routinely pore over the statistical properties of every fund: one of the measures that most excites their attention is the extent to which a fund's holdings deviate from those of the market as a whole (its so-called 'tracking error'). Bolton's funds have one of the highest 'tracking errors' of all UK equity funds.[11]

[11] Calling deviation from an index 'tracking error' is evidence of how far the concept of indexing has advanced in modern investment management: for an index fund, which is specifically designed to match the performance of an index, such deviation is indeed reprehensible. For an actively managed fund such as Special Situations, the reverse is often the case.

Whether or not contrarian stockpicking of the kind that Bolton goes in for is in reality unusually risky is a moot point, and one that is discussed elsewhere in this book. What it does mean, unquestionably, is that it places an onus on the fund manager to pick his stocks with more than average care. Mishaps and the occasional disaster are an inevitable consequence. Bolton has had his fair share of disasters along the way, including such horror stories as Polly Peck, Mountleigh and the Parkfield group, all of which either went bust or had to be rescued while in his ownership. A similar experience threatened to befall him more recently when Railtrack, the rail network operator, was threatened with effective renationalisation, a situation that was only redeemed when Fidelity and other leading shareholders banded together to take legal action against the Government. Without the strength of a broadly diversified fund, and the market clout of Fidelity behind him, these bad experiences might have proved too much for a less highly regarded manager, but Bolton is now sufficiently well established to be able to shrug off the occasional failure. He is playing a numbers game, and is confident that the gems, will on average, outnumber the duds. His ability to pick more than his fair share of winners while avoiding disasters is actually, his colleagues say, one of his greatest strengths as an investor.[12]

The shares he likes

Being an analytical sort, and being constantly required to justify his methods to potential investors in his funds, Bolton has broken down the types of special situation he wants to buy into a number of different categories, all in the general category of 'unfashionable or undervalued' stocks. This has shown some subtle changes over the years, though the underlying philosophy is unchanged. In his early reports to investors, Bolton listed eight categories: small growth stocks, recovery shares, asset situations, new issues, companies involved in bids, energy and resource stocks, companies reorganising or changing their business, and new technology companies. Now in his presentations, he has refined the list to cover six generic types of situation. The headings are recovery, unrecognised growth, valuation anomalies, corporate potential (mainly shorthand for takeover prospects), asset plays and

---

[12] See for example the comments by Alex Hammond-Chambers on page 121 and those of Lee Gardhouse on page 147.

industry arbitrage. The philosophy behind this categorisation is set out in more detail by Bolton himself in the next chapter.

Of all his many early successes, Bolton is particularly proud of his success in finding the Mersey Docks and Harbour Board. This was a classic example of a business that conventional opinion thought to be a disaster, but which turned out to be what Peter Lynch liked to call a 'tenbagger' (a share which makes investors ten times their money). For years, the Board had been lumbered with the cost of enforcing the disastrous dock labour scheme introduced by the Labour government. This guaranteed employment to all dockers in the area, whatever the state of demand. Mrs Thatcher's government ended the dock labour scheme, but left most of the companies which operated the docks with the burden of meeting the resulting redundancy payments to dockers.

What Bolton saw, but which many others did not, was that the company was sitting on a highly valuable property portfolio. When the Conservative government privatised another docks company, Associated British Ports, it wrote off most of the company's liability for its redundancy payments in order to make sure the issue was a success. Bolton took a bet that something similar would happen with the Mersey Docks and Harbour Board. He was proved right: in fact, the government wrote off 100% of its liabilities for redundancy payments, leaving a business that was both asset rich and, for the first time in years, capable of making a worthwhile profit on its activities. The shares rose tenfold in just a few years.

The 'corporate potential' category is also of note. It is not quite right to say that this is purely a euphemism for 'takeover prospects', but Bolton has never disguised his interest in trying to spot companies that are likely to experience a change in management or control. He regards this as a legitimate activity for a professional fund manager, and one that many of his professional peers unwisely neglect. He had spectacular success in buying independent television companies in the 1990s. Five of the six he bought shares in were later taken over, reflecting the industry-wide consensus that the small regional monopolies originally set up by the government could not survive in the modern age of satellite and digital technology. (More recently still, he was to play a pivotal and unexpectedly high profile part in the merger that combined the last two surviving ITV companies, Carlton and Granada, in

2003.) Privatised electricity firms were another case where he found it was possible, on general principles alone, to foresee an industry-wide round of takeovers well in advance.

The general moral for investors in his approach is that there can often be something remarkably fragrant lurking behind a bad smell, provided you are prepared to go and sniff it out. Not all companies that perform badly are necessarily beyond redemption. The trick for a contrarian investor is to put yourself in the way of interesting ideas of this kind, where you can see the potential for change and also have a chance to get in early enough to take advantage of the change before it is fully recognised by the market as a whole. "My experience", says Bolton, "is that most investors tend to avoid companies that have not done well recently, and this reaction creates the buying opportunity". More recently, the much increased size and clout of the fund means that Bolton's emergence on a company's share register often now leaves him in a powerful position to promote or block changes in a company's ownership. In underperforming companies, where he has a major stake, he has become more of an agent for change, and less of a passive investor.

Casting the net wide

In his early days running the fund, Bolton had little internal research to fall back on and says that most of his ideas came from brokers, something that his early notebooks reflect. Early reports to fundholders note approvingly that Fidelity had relationships with more than fifty London and regional stockbrokers, the latter especially useful for analysing small local companies.[13] Even then, however, he liked to cast the net quite widely. "I have always worked on the basis of having lots of ideas put to you from many sources and then choosing quite selectively from them. It is like a big sieving process. You get all these ideas brought to you, and then you choose just a few of them." He still uses a lot of broking material now, despite Fidelity's own extensive in-house research capability. That is partly because it is impossible to cover every stock across such a wide universe, but it also stems from an innate belief that it pays investors to expose themselves to as many new ideas as possible.

---

[13] For example, the Special Situations Trust's report May 1981.

HOW FIDELITY SPECIAL SITUATIONS HAS GROWN
Total net assets 1987-2004

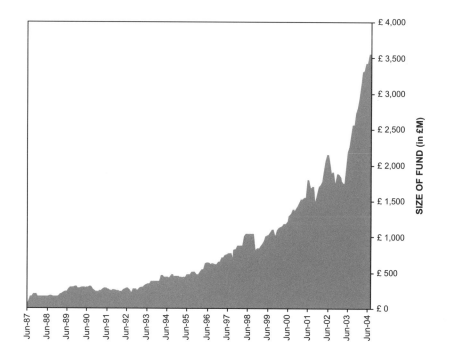

The trouble with relying on brokers is, says Bolton, "they tend to be good at getting you into something but aren't so good at getting you out of it. If they get you into something that doesn't go that well, then they tend to lose interest in helping you to follow it. Time was when they thought something was a buy, they would tell a few of their favoured clients first. Now the regulators insist that they have to tell everyone at the same time, so there is a sort of scramble and if it is a very good idea, a few people get in and the bigger clients don't." The trick for a big investor such as Fidelity, even when it has a good idea, is therefore to find a way of getting in, and getting out, of shares earlier than the market as a whole. These days the firm has a dedicated trading desk to execute the orders that Bolton and all the other fund managers place, but the issue of managing liquidity remains an ever present one – not least because, given the scale of its operations today, Fidelity can quickly become the largest single shareholder in the small and midcap companies that he favours.

23

As a result, moving in and out of stocks is no longer as easy as it once was for Bolton, at least in the UK market. As his funds have grown in size, his choice has been between sticking to his last, hunting for small out of fashion stocks and simply looking for more of them, or changing his approach and looking for value among bigger quoted companies instead. Since the mid 1990s, when the fund catapulted in size to become the largest single fund of its kind, he has opted to take both approaches. In the main he continues to prefer to stick in the small and midcap area of the market, partly because that is the way that Lynch and others in Fidelity have tended to do it. But he is equally happy to own more stocks in the upper reaches of the market when valuations appear attractive, as they began to do, for example, he found, towards the end of 2003.

Sticking to the same value-driven discipline with a much larger portfolio makes it even more important to be able to work closely with a team of analysts and fund managers. "I really need the team to help monitor all the two hundred or so stocks that are now in the portfolios. In fact, the primary thing that the analysts do for me is help monitor what I own." The growing size of the fund, Bolton says, must put something of a drag on his future performance, though not disastrously so. "It means I am not so likely to see my fund appearing in the top decile of the performance tables, but my target is still to be in the top quartile, and there is no question in my mind that this is achievable."[14] The question whether the fund has grown too big to be able to produce above average returns in future is one that continues to exercise the many financial advisers whose clients have done so well out of Bolton's expertise.[15] Fidelity's range of funds is carefully managed, but no other individual fund manager has done as well for so long, and news of his successor, when the time finally comes, will be keenly awaited.

Why does investing in recovery stocks, and all the other out of favour categories he likes, seem to work so well? It comes back, in Bolton's view, to the herdlike behaviour of the market. "You have got to use the excesses of

---

[14] For those not familiar with the commonly used parlance of fund management, a fund is in the top decile if its performance ranks in the top 10% of similar funds: and in the top quartile if it ranks amongst the top 25% of its peers.

[15] Questioned about the size issue, Bolton told the Sunday Telegraph in November 2003: "I do believe there is a point when a fund becomes unmanageable, but I'm not sure exactly what it is."

the stock market to your advantage. Looking at recovery stocks forces you to go against the herd. Most people feel confident doing what the herd's doing. If everyone tells them Vodafone is a good company, then they want to believe that Vodafone is a good company. If three brokers ring me and tell me something is a buy, then I normally say "that doesn't look too good". The market is excessive. It gets too optimistic on things and then gets too pessimistic on things. I also think it is quite short term and won't look at things like the longer-term dynamics of a business."

The key thing any serious investor must have is an information advantage over the rest of the market. "Generally I would feel uncomfortable taking a view on some of the macroeconomic stuff, and on things like oil prices. Why should I have a better view than hundreds of other people on them? But if you are looking at a small company in particular, there are times when you come out of some of our meetings with companies, and you can say, 'Gosh, I probably know more about this company than anyone else at this moment'. It is Jim Slater's Zulu Principle at work: if you are the expert on something, however small it may be in the broader context of things, you have an advantage over other people.[16] I want to put my bets on things where I have some advantage over others. We're also using the power of Fidelity as one of the biggest investors in the world to get access to companies and information. I am not talking about inside information, but about lots of little bits of things that when you put them together gives you a better informed view than the average investor."[17]

Getting rich in Europe

One of the notable things about Bolton's career is that he has managed to demonstrate that his stockpicking methods can work in two distinct investment arenas. Very few fund managers succeed in running an active equity portfolio in both the UK and European markets simultaneously, as he has done. (Nils Taube is one, but there are not many others.) Bolton's early interest in European stocks can be explained in part by his desire to be looking

---

[16] Jim Slater was a high-flying financier in the bull market before last, the one that ended in the late 1960s/early 1970s. His credo, dubbed the Zulu Principle after a remark by his wife, has always been that the way to success is to know a lot about a little.

[17] Under modern insider trading laws, it is illegal to buy or sell shares on the basis of information which is not publicly available.

for shares where other investors are not. "I started getting interested in Europe in the early 1980s. For somebody who likes unresearched stocks, Europe was amazing at that time, because it was completely undercovered. The stock markets were very unsophisticated in the way they reacted to news. Now that has changed dramatically; not completely, but it has changed dramatically."

Traditionally, fund managers had tended to regard the UK and Europe as quite distinct sectors. "You put your linguists onto Continental Europe", he recalls, "but it was very much the poor relation. Your best people were in the UK, America and Japan, and then Continental Europe was last." The combination of unsophisticated markets and limited competition made Europe look a good bet at the time, though Bolton adds: "As I was useless at languages, I was probably the last person who should have been put onto Europe. But at least I knew a bit about investment, so I was able to spot things that others had not."

There are good reasons why European stocks are harder for investors trained in the UK to analyse than their American or British counterparts. Accounting conventions are different, for example; the level of information disclosure has historically been less good; and in countries such as France, there are often complex cross-holdings and ownership structures to resolve as well. If you think earnings figures are unreliable in the UK, then the figures reported by Continental companies are much worse. Bolton therefore prefers to rely on other types of valuation ratio, such as the ratio of enterprise value to cash flow, in preference to conventional price/earnings ratios.[18] This, he points out, is how most companies value each other when weighing up whether or not to make a take-over bid which makes it a useful tool for investors too – especially ones who, like Bolton, are interested in spotting potential bid targets.

The way Fidelity goes about analysing European shares is to compare sector valuations from one country to another. "Someone will look at, say, the food retailers here, Sainsburys and Tesco, and then compare the valuations with the Carrefour, and so on, on the Continent. I believe that if you are looking at an Italian insurance company, you want to look at it first through the eyes

---

[18] To work out an enterprise to cash flow ratio, you take the economic value of the company - the market capitalisation of its shares and its net debt, added together – and divide it by gross cash flow (roughly speaking, operating profit plus depreciation).

FIDELITY EUROPEAN 1985-2002
Value of £1,000 invested at launch

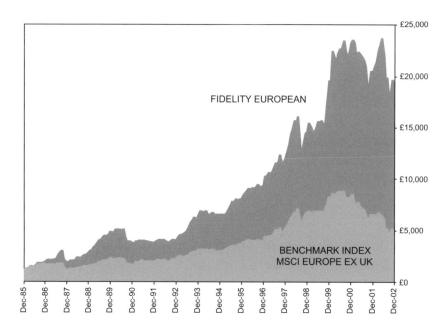

of someone who knows about insurance, and only later through the eyes of someone who knows all about Italy. The things you have learnt in the more sophisticated markets such as the UK and America help you to spot anomalies and opportunities in Europe. That is generally what I try to do." Sometimes the trend actually works the other way round. Bolton bought shares in British Energy, the privatised company which runs the country's nuclear power stations, not just because other investors were reluctant to buy – 'nuclear' being a classic 'bad smell' word – but because similar European utilities were trading on higher multiples and there was less of a 'nuclear discount'.

Wherever he is investing, Bolton has always been careful not to base the case for owning the shares he buys on broad macroeconomic grounds alone. (In the same way he makes little attempt to try and time the market.) In economic terms, he once told me, the macro argument for being an owner of European equities, for example, was "not that great". He reckoned that the drive towards federalism in Europe was actually quite negative for growth. But that was counterbalanced in the early years by the structural changes which have made equities more popular on the Continent, and companies much more open in the amount of information that they will disclose to investors. German companies, says Bolton, are the only ones which still adopt the traditional Continental habit of refusing to see investors who want to come and visit them, but even that is now slowly changing for the better.

Bolton's European portfolios were run on broadly the same principles as his UK ones, but with a greater bias towards larger companies. The primary emphasis was still on small and medium-sized companies, with a market capitalisation in the £50 million to £500 million range, but there was a large leavening (about 25% of the portfolio) of leading companies too. He says he found there were fewer turnaround situations than in the UK but more companies selling at a discount to their asset value. One reason for this is that the potential for takeover is much greater in the UK than in most European countries. Companies which sell at a discount to their asset value for too long are liable to find themselves bid for in the UK market. By contrast, contested takeovers are much rarer on the Continent, where banks, rather than institutional investors, are the dominant shareholders. The main thing that differentiated him from the competition is that his approach is resolutely bottom-up. Many other European funds are run on asset allocation grounds – so much in France, so much in Germany – but Bolton's funds are driven almost exclusively by where he finds the best value.

As a result, the shape of his funds looked very different to that of his average competitor: for much of the 1990s, for example, they were heavily weighted towards Scandinavian countries. This is partly, he says now, because companies in the northern countries of Europe are more willing to talk to investors, and to take shareholder interests into account, than they are in, say, France or Italy. But it also reinforces the basic premise that Bolton brings to his investment approach: namely, that if you do the same as everybody else, then you will end up performing just the same way. In fact, it would be an affront to Bolton's entire philosophy if he found that his portfolios had the same weightings as the rest of his competitors. They rarely do, as the analysis by outside fund analysts repeatedly demonstrates.[19]

He does however keep an eye on the overall balance of the portfolio to make sure that is has not become too reliant on any one theme or market; in his

---

[19] See the report on the Fidelity Special Values investment trust by analysts at Close Winterflood Securities for an example (page 158).

European funds, for example, with the exception of the major markets (Germany, France, Switzerland and Holland), no other country ever exceeded 20% of the total. The same goes for his UK funds, where his weightings in the various market sectors, regularly recorded in his funds' annual reports, bear only a tangential relationship to the market as a whole. He sees no point in trying to stack the odds against himself by filling his funds with shares in one sector, just because that is what everyone else is doing, when he would rather be buying more attractively priced shares in another. Except in very exceptional circumstances, however, such as the height of the bull market in 1999-2000, when he owned virtually nothing in the modish TMT sectors, it is rare for him to have no exposure at all to a sector. The main way that Bolton manages risk in his portfolios is by making sure that no single bet can put his whole fund at risk: it is unusual for any holding to exceed 3% of the total fund, or for him to be more than 30% 'overweight' in any one sector.

Looking beyond the UK

Although he has now given up his European responsibilities, the legacy of his time running money outside the boundaries of the UK persists. The UK Special Situations fund has always had a remit that allows him to invest up to 20% of the fund outside the UK; and the opportunity is one of which Bolton has regularly taken advantage. Indeed, although he only occasionally approaches the 20% threshold these days, in the 1980s he sometimes had as much as 25% in holdings classified as being outside the UK at balance sheet date. The early reports by the Special Situations Trust are punctuated by the sudden emergence of obscure overseas companies that subsequently disappear as fast as they appear. In September 1981, for example, he had more than 5% of the fund in both Norway and Australia, mainly in the form of oil and mining stocks. Five years later a crop of Italian shares appear fleetingly in the portfolio. At another point he is reported to have been buying Eurobond warrants. In the 1990s Bolton again built up positions in Norwegian oil companies; and more recently, he has taken advantage of the economic boom in China to invest in a number of companies there.

Although it inevitably confounds the thought police in the investment consultancy world, whose sophisticated analytical models depend on the funds they analyse displaying so-called 'style purity', the ability to invest in other areas adds a further moneymaking dimension to Bolton's armoury. His rationale is simple: "Investing in other countries is something that I have always done. It fits in with my style and has served the fundholders well. There is no reason not to go on doing so, particularly where I have a special knowledge of a market or industry."[20] That said, he emphasises that the overseas stocks he buys are almost always those that aren't well followed by other analysts, or ones where he believes he can bring some kind of personal competitive advantage to bear. Although he has occasionally owned some American stocks they won't be well-known names, but smaller companies that typically may have a particular British angle – for example, Cadiz Inc, a Californian company that owns water rights in the United States and is listed on an American stock exchange, but was mainly financed by British investors and is run by a British CEO. By the same token, when he owned shares in TNT, the Australian transport company, 80% of its business was in Europe at the time.

His years of tramping round Europe, calling on companies means that he still has a solid core of knowledge on which to draw, and he has increased his holdings of European shares in his UK funds since giving up responsibility for Fidelity's European funds. They continue to add a bit of spice to the portfolio. His interest in China, meanwhile, is driven in part by a bargain-hunter's sense of value, but also by a feeling that this is now the most promising part of the world for any investor to be looking for new stocks. In the autumn of 2004, he spent two weeks in China and Hong Kong, visiting some forty companies. Shortly afterwards he also paid a visit to India.[21] His verdict: "China interests me for three reasons. One is that it is one of the most exciting places that I have come across in recent times to find new stocks. The second is that China has become such an important factor in determining what happens to the rest of the world from an investment perspective. Going there and finding out what is happening on the ground gives me a good chance of establishing an advantage over other investors. Finally, having given up my European responsibilities, learning about a new area is itself a new mental challenge, something to keep me interested and on my toes."

---

[20] That said, the non-UK exposure makes it harder to make fair comparisons between his fund and that of other UK equity funds, which may be 100% invested in the UK.

[21] Fidelity launched both a Chinese and an Indian fund in October 2004.

Fidelity has a local research team based in the Far East, and Bolton has been using his experience of watching the European markets develop to help them spot the companies that he believes have the greatest potential for the future. The biggest risk for investors in China is not finding attractive buying opportunities, he says, but the corporate governance system (that is, the answer to the question "Will you get your money back?") is not as certain as it could be. This is one reason why the few investments Bolton has made to date are mostly in firms that have established Western partners. The Chinese stocks remain a modest proportion of his overall portfolio. He says, surprisingly, that he has never stopped to work out whether his overseas holdings have contributed materially to his performance over the years.

Where the ideas come from

Bolton says that his ideas rarely come as bolts from the blue, but accumulate in his mind until he has a conviction that something is the right thing to buy or sell. You need both knowledge of what constitutes a good company and an insight into how a company of its type should be valued. It is then a question of spotting anomalies, assimilating new information as it comes in and waiting for convictions to develop. "Conviction waxes and wanes and a lot of the time you're uncertain about everything, but when you do get a strong conviction, then it is important to back it strongly." In other words, when he feels strongly that he has found a winner, he will put a lot of money behind it, even if that means making his funds more heavily concentrated than many of his rivals. Even so, unless a large line of shares suddenly becomes available, his normal style is to build his positions in stages, testing the water with an initial purchase and then, if the market action supports his idea, to add to it as his conviction grows. He freely confesses that he is not always sure, even after making a sizeable investment, that he has done the right thing. "Some seem to think people like myself are hugely sure about what they are doing all the time", he told an interviewer in 2002, "but this business is not like that. You are in a constant state of questioning your convictions."[22]

---

[22] Citywire Funds Insider April 2002. He also said in this interview: "Investment is a funny combination of being flexible and open-minded at times, and at others having the conviction to back something you feel is mis-priced and undervalued."

Unlike 'buy and hold' investors, who like to hold shares for long periods, Bolton's policy is normally to sell shares as soon as they have become fully valued. At that point, it is time to move on to something else. His normal time frame for an investment is one to two years, though in exceptional cases (such as Securicor) it may be much longer. That helps to explain why turnover in his portfolios is reasonably high: something like 70% of the portfolio turns over every year. His average holding period for a share is 18 months. This is what comes from being an investor who looks for pricing anomalies and draws his ideas from so many sources. It is not the style of, say, Ian Rushbrook.[23] Nevertheless, when I asked Bolton who had influenced him most as an investor, the first name he mentioned was Warren Buffett, even though the latter's style as an investor could not be more different. Although he owns nothing like as many stocks and deals only rarely, Buffett was responsible, says Bolton, for implanting in him two ideas: the value of companies with strong business franchises, and the value of businesses that are capable of generating free cash flow.

He also says he takes on board 'a lot of the Peter Lynch approach', which he defined as 'hands-on investment, seeing the companies, the strong view that if you predict earnings, you predict share prices'. Finally, he also echoed Nils Taube's view that, in one sense, the game of successful professional investment is also about plagiarism: looking for good ideas that other people have had, and copying them like mad when you find them. Rather like the stocks he buys, which come in all shapes and sizes, Bolton has something of a 'Smorgasbord approach' when it comes to articulating the major influences of his investment style. There is, for example, an obvious tension between his desire to be a contrarian and his willingness to look at charts to see what other investors have been buying and selling. And although he is known, and regards himself as a 'value investor', he clearly also has a keen eye for a company that others might more readily classify as 'growth stock'.[24]

---

[23] Ian Rushbrook is the investment director of the Personal Assets investment trust in Edinburgh, a fund for private investors that is characterised by a long term approach. In most years he only makes four or five changes in his portfolio, on the basis that it pays to get a few good decisions rights rather than a lot of poor ones wrong.

[24] In reality, the line between 'growth' and 'value' is a blurred one – a fast growing company can offer value by being too lowly rated, even though it fails to meet the conventional value stock criteria such as an above average dividend yield, or a low price to book value. One of Bolton's greatest successes was spotting Nokia long before it became a world leading mobile phone company.

Using technical analysis

Bolton is unusual among top-class investors in admitting quite happily that he has always used a lot of technical analysis, or charts, to support his investment analysis. A chartist in investment terms is someone who attempts to predict future winners and losers in the stock market by analysing the past performance of shares, using a variety of techniques which vary, quite literally, from the sublime to the ridiculous. The rationale for technical analysis is that it is possible to make deductions about the next movement in a share's price from the information contained in its recent price history. From the early days of Mister Johnson, Fidelity has always recognised that technical analysis has a place in an investor's armoury, so much so that all its investment management offices, including the London one, have chart rooms where scores of printed charts, some almost as big as plate glass windows, are displayed on banks of wooden screens ranged around the walls.

What chartists look for, typically, are common patterns which they believe signal a future change in a share's direction. Many investors regard this form of investment analysis as dangerous nonsense, although it has a long history and has proved remarkably resilient. The American writer and investment counsellor John Train speaks for most of the sceptics when he says, "I find charting as a matter of practical experience to be useless." Thirty years ago, Jim Slater won an easy laugh from his audiences by observing that chartists usually had "dirty raincoats and large overdrafts". The conventional thing to ask is: 'When did you last see one who looks rich?'

But Bolton is not so sceptical.[25] He uses charts to help screen out possible buying ideas, and as an early warning signal that something may be going wrong at a company he already owns. He finds technical analysis particularly useful when looking at large companies, as he increasingly has to do, given the size of his funds. Glaxo SmithKline is a good example. It is a world-class drugs company, and a leading blue chip share, but its shares, Bolton notes, are unusually volatile for such a large company. It goes from being "very in favour to very out of favour", even though the fundamentals of the business are well known. Looking at the charts on companies such as Glaxo often

---

[25] Nor actually now is Slater. He too says there is value to be had in looking at charts to see how the balance between buyers and sellers is shaping up.

Bolton: very much at home in the Fidelity chartroom

gives Bolton a first clue about when it is about to move into a new phase of its cycle. He has experimented with a number of different services over the years, but now relies mainly on Fidelity's own in-house technical analysts and an American service, QAS, for international stocks. The great advantage of the American service is that it routinely classifies where in the cycle the charts suggest each of the leading stocks in its universe has reached.

One day when I was in his office, Bolton gave me two topical examples of how charts had helped his thinking. One was the French computer company Axime, which he had owned for some time. It looked reasonably valued compared to other international computer companies. As he liked the sector, it was a stock he would normally have been looking to buy more of, but the charts suggested that the shares were in the process of 'topping out' on technical grounds, and this had made him cautious instead. A second example was the French television company TF1. Having owned it for ages, not only had the Fidelity in-house analyst turned negative on the shares, but the charts were also suggesting that the technical position of the shares was deteriorating. So Bolton had sold out of his position completely. The reason why charts do have some value, he explains, is that they give important clues about the current balance of advantage between buyers and sellers: they are the footprints which investors have left behind them.

Coping with setbacks

Despite his spectacular long term record, described in detail in a later section of this book, life has not always gone smoothly for Bolton as an investor. His biggest setback came in the 1990-91 recession, when his funds suddenly started to perform very badly. His run until then had been quite spectacular. In its first ten years, the Special Situations fund clocked up a cumulative return of more than 1,000%, a pace that was clearly unsustainable. The fund recorded nine years of positive returns out of ten: not only that, the nine good calendar years all delivered an annual return of more than 23%, an incredible run, even for a roaring bull market (not least because the decade included 1987, the year when Wall Street fell by a quarter in just a few days).[26] Ironically enough, because the fund's reporting period never ran to the end of the calendar year, and the movement in the fund's asset value was quite volatile, Bolton's reports to shareholders are surprisingly often taken up with explaining away shorter periods of relatively poor results. By chance, one of the fund's reports appeared in October 1987, only days before so-called 'Black Monday', with this hapless statement: "Although valuation levels are high and the poor performance of gilts is a cause for concern, at the moment we believe the bull market is not yet over." In one sense, this was correct: the market did make a strong recovery from the October 1987 crash and the bull market powered on for anther two years, but the timing could have been better.[27]

By the start of the 1990s however, a recession did hit both the UK economy and the financial markets hard. In 1990, the fund lost 28.8% of its value in a year, a bad hit. In 1991, the return was a positive one, but only just (3.0%). A number of Bolton's holdings, instead of recovering from the economic downturn, as he had expected, simply went bust on him instead. Fund

[26] Bolton describes his personal experience of the extraordinary events of October 1987 in the next chapter (page 58).

[27] The statement nonetheless underlines the dangers in making forward market projections, something Bolton usually tries to avoid wherever possible.

management, being a highly competitive business, can also be rather bitchy, and there were a lot of mutterings around the City that the great Bolton, whose reputation as the best performing manager in his sector was by then already known, had lost his touch. For the first time in its history, the fund's five-year performance record fell behind that of the FTSE All-Share Index. In its October 1991 report, Fidelity reported: "The last six months have continued to be a very depressing period for investors in this Trust and they are owed a detailed explanation of why this was the case and what went wrong. In the last report we wrote that we believed a new strong upward trend or 'bull phase' had started in the UK market and that – as in past cycles – it had started in the recession and before the recovery is clear..... We were too early in identifying a better environment for the type of company which accounts for the majority of the portfolio." One shareholder was so disgruntled at the decline in the fund's fortunes that he wrote to tell Bolton that his performance was so bad that he ought to be outside "sweeping the streets", a comment that is now immortalised in a cartoon on the wall of his office.

Bolton, who is nothing but his own harshest critic, conceded later that this was his toughest period. In hindsight, the downturn of 1990-1991 can be seen for what it proved to be, namely an 18-month setback on the way to a renewed long run of future superior performance. At the time it was nothing like so obvious. "I did a lot of soul searching in the early 1990s, when I had a bad patch", he told me in 1998, "If you hit a bad economic recession, it is obviously bad for my type of investing. But the question was: should I change my approach or not? Thank goodness, I didn't, because that would have been the kiss of death. If you start doing a type of investment that you don't feel confident in, that's where you become completely unstuck." Since then, he and his colleagues at Fidelity have put a lot more effort into tracking 'z scores' and other tools used by credit analysts for spotting potential corporate failures.[28] The implication at the time was that Bolton had been skimping a bit on his homework. He denies that charge, but admits that he has learnt a lot from his experience at the time.

---

[28] 'z scores' are composite ratios which analyse the strength or weakness of a company's finances and have been shown to be very successful at highlighting impending insolvencies.

MOSTLY, NOT ALWAYS SUPERIOR
Difference in rolling 3-year returns
Fidelity Special Situations vs FTSE All-Share Index

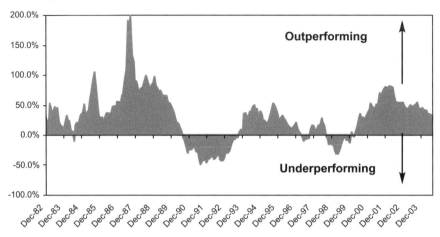

After a spectacular beginning, Special Situations underperformed the market in 1990-1992 and again in 1997-1998

His argument was then, and has been ever since, that the above average-volatility of his funds is something that both he and his investors simply have to learn to live with. "In recession, the kind of medium-sized companies that I invest in will often fall further than the big cap companies. It is a price that I have to pay. There is little I can do about it." His attitude now, he told me, is: "I don't mind buying a high risk, badly financed company provided I know the business well. It was the few where the finances were far worse than we realised that hurt us. We don't want to make that mistake again. That is why we do a lot more balance sheet work now." Another reason why his shares underperformed so badly during the 1990-91 recession may ironically, he thinks now, have been a result of the Fidelity policy of staying close to the companies they own. What made that particular recession different from previous ones was that even the companies which suffered most from the economic change were taken aback by the scale of the downturn. There was, for example, no cluster of share sales by directors which is what you would normally expect if the companies had been fully aware of what was about to hit them.

But while he is open about the above average volatility of his funds, he has come to the conclusion that "I have an approach that delivers in the medium and longer term. Why mess it up because once in a while people have an uncomfortable period?"[29] In any case, he says, good investment managers should not be over sensitive about their failures. Taking their lumps is part of the business. "You have to be comfortable in taking a different view from most other people. Most people like it if five people tell them they're right – that makes them feel more confident. I am not a very emotional person, and I think that's the only way you can run money. You've got to be very unemotional about stocks, and you have to be prepared to say you were wrong. This is the sort of business where you get bitten by the bug. It's constantly changing, constantly challenging. You must change with the changing climate, and not fall in love with what worked last year or the year before. Just as importantly, you need the support of an employer who is prepared to ride over the lumpy periods."[30]

The bull market and beyond

In the event, the 1990s proved to be a good, though not the best, decade of Bolton's career. Perhaps it had something to do with the fact that he was by now running two large pools of money, one for European stocks and the other his UK funds, but there were times when Bolton's UK funds, measured by their rolling three and five year performance, for once failed to beat their benchmarks by a handsome margin. True, investors in the Special Situations fund still had good cause to be happy, as their absolute returns were invariably positive. The average five-year return on the fund for investors who joined since January 1990 has been 119%, against 70% for the FTSE All-Share Index. But style trends in the market do not always favour Bolton's approach, and his relative performance, in the UK at least, suffered for a while, not least towards the end of the bull market when euphoria reached a new and unsustainable peak.

In 1998, Bolton told me in an interview for Institutional Investor magazine that he could not recall a time in his career when small and medium company shares, of the kind he favours, were so shunned by other investors – or so attractively valued for a bargain-hunting investor. He was right, but the market being as always a slave to fashion, and soon to be bewitched by the

---

[29] Interview with Bloomberg, January 1997.

30 Quoted in Financial Adviser, October 1991.

wonders of the internet craze, investors studiously ignored him for nearly 18 months. The discount on his investment trust, a barometer of his fund's standing in the eyes of the market, widened to an unprecedented 25%, creating a rare (and so far unrepeated) opportunity for savvy investors to buy into his stockpicking skills on the cheap. Shares in the investment trust, which owns almost exactly the same shares as the Special Situations unit trust, went to a premium in 2001 and have rarely gone to a discount since. Over the five years to the end of 2003, the unit trust produced a return of 120% and the investment trust 168%, in a period when the market itself, reeling from the bear market, lost 5% of its value.

In fact, the way that Bolton's funds have performed since the end of the great bull market has revealed another side to his talents as an investor. While he made his name by outperforming the market on the way up, his performance since the market peaked in March 2000 has, if anything, been even more creditable. It has certainly reinforced his reputation. As we now know, the pricing of the internet bubble, and the associated fashion for 'TMT stocks' (telecom, media and technology shares), was followed by the severest bear market for a generation. From its peak in March 2000 to its nadir in March 2003, the UK stock market, as measured by the FTSE All-Share Index, fell by nearly 50%. The great majority of actively managed equity funds tanked with it.

Many of the managers whose funds had soared in the last stages of the bull market turned out to be paper tigers, or one-trick ponies; scores of aggressively managed funds lost 70% or more of their investors' money. By rights Bolton's fund too, being of above average risk according to conventional classifications, should have suffered more than the market. Yet Fidelity Special Situations, while not immune from the market decline, has suffered nothing like as much, as these figures show. In fact, his was one of only a handful of funds that managed to produce a positive return over the period March 2000 - March 2003:[31]

---

[31] The difference between the fall in the FTSE All-Share Index of nearly 50% and the total return loss of 39.3% shown in the table is accounted for by dividends. In this book all comparisons between the performance of Fidelity Special Situations (which does not pay a dividend) and the FTSE All-Share Index (many of whose component companies do) are adjusted for dividends to ensure a like-for-like comparison.

	BOLTON	MARKET	DIFFERENCE
MID 1990s BULL MARKET March 1993 - March 1996	73.2%	48.5%	24.7%
LATE BULL MARKET March 1996 - March 1999	40.3%	71.2%	-30.9%
LAST YEAR OF BULL MARKET March 1999 - March 2000	29.3%	9.9%	19.4%
BEAR MARKET March 2000 - March 2003	3.8%	-39.3%	43.1%
RECOVERY March 2003 - August 2004	58.9%	34.0%	24.9%

There are a number of reasons, Bolton says, why his performance has continued to be so strong. One can be traced back to the months before the market peaked, when shares in three sectors of the market, telecommunications, technology and media, all loosely and indiscriminately linked to the emergence of the internet, were so 'hot' that their valuations lost all touch with reality. At one point these three sectors accounted for some 40% of the entire value of the UK stock market. Yet Bolton owned virtually none of them: refusing to abandon his value disciplines, he was quietly loading up on scores of other shares whose prices had been untouched by the market bubble, and indeed were trading at what, historically, were absurdly low ratings.

That led his fund to lag the market at the time, but ensured that once the bubble burst, his performance would recover strongly. Alex Hammond-Chambers, the chairman of Fidelity Special Values, thinks this was one of Bolton's finest hours. "At the time, there was nothing unusual about having nearly half your portfolio in the TMT stocks, because that was where the index was and everybody else was doing it. But if you want to be a special investor, and you are naturally risk-averse, you have got to do what you believe is right, and absolutely not be swayed by the herd. Most fund managers are lemmings, and Anthony is the absolute antithesis of a lemming." In particular he did not fall into the trap of thinking that just because a stock in the most favoured sectors was trading on half the price-earnings multiple of the market leaders, it had therefore to be cheap. As it turned out, even the 'cheapest' stocks in the TMT arena were grossly overvalued.

A second reason why the UK funds have done so well since the bull market ended is that value investing as a discipline, having been increasingly overlooked as investors chased ever more improbable technology-fuelled growth stories during the boom, came back into fashion. Almost overnight shares that paid dividends and enjoyed high dividend yields, or traded on low multiples of earnings or book value, the classic value criteria, started to come back into favour. As a value-minded investor, Bolton was always likely to do relatively well in this climate. At the same time, the period since 2000 has been one in which small and medium-sized companies as a group have, for the most part, outperformed larger stocks. This too has helped Bolton's performance, as did the fact that in 1999 an exceptionally large number of stocks in his portfolio were taken over.

Even so, to outperform the market and his peers so handsomely during the bear market underlines that his success is anything but a bull market phenomenon. Although he insists that he is primarily a stockpicker, not a market timer, Bolton has since shown too that he has developed an informed better nose for the currents that are running through the market. In March 2003, to the surprise of his audience at the time, who had mostly never heard him offer such a definitive view on the market before, he correctly called the bottom of the bear market, almost to the day. This was no idle comment either. A few weeks earlier he had, it turns out, suggested to the board of his investment trust, Fidelity Special Values, that it would be a good moment to consider increasing the amount of gearing in the fund to take advantage of an expected upturn in the market.[32]

Into the limelight: the ITV saga

Bolton has always taken care to develop and sustain good relationships with financial advisers and the media, recognising that there are the two external groups that have the most influence over the direction of fund flows in the UK. While he responds regularly to requests to give interviews and presentations, it would be wrong to describe him as a publicity-seeker. Though happy to talk about the markets and his current thinking, it is not his style to gossip about his competitors, or to use the media to talk up the shares in his fund, as some professional investors have been known to do. That kind of approach does not sit easily with his character. When he does talk to

---

[32] Bolton made his remarks at a seminar for financial advisers organised by Jupiter Asset Management (at which the author was present). It is not clear whether he realised that his prediction was going to be reported in the media. I suspect not.

outsiders, he tends to err on the side of caution, being measured to the point sometimes of blandness in his comments about companies and their managers.

Those who know him well were therefore somewhat surprised to find his name being spread all over the business news pages in the summer of 2003 as the alleged leader of 'a plot' to oust the leaders of the two largest surviving independent television companies, Carlton and Granada. According to the Sunday Times, in a front page story in its business section, "the City's most respected fund manager" was canvassing the television industry for candidates to replace both Michael Green, the chairman of Carlton, and Charles Allen, his counterpart at Granada, when the two companies merged. The merger was something that the two companies had announced they were planning to do a few weeks earlier. The paper went on to quote an unnamed City analyst describing Bolton as "the City's quiet assassin".

It was a vivid phrase, one that helped to give the story a striking headline. In reality, Bolton's stance was at that stage merely that of the concerned shareholder. He had been an investor in both Carlton and Granada since at least 2001. "I did not propose the idea of merger between the two companies, but once it had been aired as a possibility, I was definitely in favour", is how he recalls the matter now. "There were some obvious inefficiencies in the existing ITV structure, and I could see that the merger was capable of bringing great benefits, provided that it was structured in the right way." Over a period of weeks he talked to a number of people in the media industry to canvas their views on who should best run ITV if the merger of Carlton and Granada was to go through. He had not at this stage, he says, talked to any other shareholders in the two companies concerned. The story of what the paper chose to call Bolton's "back-room plotting" was leaked to the Sunday Times by a senior figure in the media industry, for reasons that remain unknown.

The biggest hurdle to any merger at that stage was whether or not the Competition Commission, to whom the matter had been referred, would allow the two largest ITV companies to put their businesses together. When he raised his concerns with the companies or their advisers, their line, Bolton recalls, was always that raising issues about the structure of the new merged company while the commission was still debating the issue would "rock the boat". It could even threaten the chances of a deal taking place. Once the initial story came out,

Bolton therefore opted to keep his counsel until the Competition Commission had reached its decision, something he now rather regrets, while continuing to canvas opinion in private. Fidelity put out a carefully worded press release after the Sunday Times story, saying that it supported the merger proposal 'in all respects', but pointedly (in its own opinion, at least) saying nothing specific about the management issue.*

It was not until the autumn of 2003, when the Commission finally cleared the idea of a merger, that Bolton and his colleagues decided to press the issue of who would run the company in the event of a merger going through. The proposal from the two companies was that the top jobs should be shared between the top executives of each company, with Michael Green, chairman of Carlton, taking the chairman's job in the new company, and Charles Allen of Granada, becoming chief executive. There was a general recognition, says Bolton, that if any changes to the proposed management of the company were going to be made, they would have to be agreed before the listing particulars for the newly merged company were finalised. Time was therefore short. The need for urgency, coupled with the strength of some of the personalities involved, played a part in turning what began as a serious but not terminal point of difference into a headline-grabbing showdown between the two companies and their leading institutional shareholders, all played out in a blaze of media publicity.

Although Bolton was the first person inside Fidelity to express concerns about the management of the merged entity, he was by no means the only player involved. Other fund managers in the Fidelity stable also owned sizeable shareholdings in the two companies, and it quickly became a matter for the company's senior management team as a whole to handle. When Fidelity went to talk to the non-executive directors of the two companies, Bolton was typically accompanied by Simon Fraser, the chief investment officer, and Trelawny Williams, the recently appointed director responsible for corporate governance. In fact, at one meeting that the trio attended, Fraser recalls, Bolton said nothing at all, somewhat scotching the idea that he was the sole driving force behind an activist shareholder plot.

---

* William Lewis, editor of the Sunday Times business section, disputes that the statement could be read as anything other than a denial that Fidelity was seeking management changes.

The battle intensifies

What is not in dispute is that the non-executive directors of the ITV companies expressed doubt at their meetings with Fidelity whether its reservations were in fact shared by other shareholders. It was only at that point, says Bolton, that he and his colleagues set out to canvas the views of other large institutional shareholders. Fidelity's contacts with several other institutions revealed that there was near-universal support for his views about the undesirability of Green and Allen splitting the top jobs between them. The two men were known not to be huge admirers of each other and could hardly have been more different in personality and behaviour. The proposed board structure looked, as it clearly was, a compromise that owed more to realpolitik than to the best interests of the merged business. Bolton and his Fidelity colleagues thought it imperative that there should be an independent non-executive chairman instead, capable of holding the ring between the two merger partners. This view was relayed back to the two companies, both directly in meetings with the non-executive directors, and indirectly through the companies' banking and broking advisers.

All this while the business sections of the national newspapers, having spotted a good story in the making, continued to give the ITV saga prominent coverage. To Bolton's irritation, they continued to present the issue in a highly personalised way, making out that he was using his position as a leading shareholder to pursue a personal vendetta against the ITV companies' top management. The 'quiet assassin' epithet, once coined, proved hard to shake off. This was far from fair, though doubtless it suited the other shareholders involved to allow Fidelity to take most of the heat. Inside Fidelity, the issue of how to deal with this unexpected publicity attracted a lot of head-scratching. Making waves in public is most definitely not the house style, though in retrospect it is not easy to see how the publicity that surrounded the ITV story could have done anything but enhance the firm's reputation. Bolton was careful to say throughout that there was nothing personal in his attempts to block the original proposals. If Allen rather than Green had been proposed as chairman, he would still have sought the appointment of an independent chairman from outside the business.

In the end, when it came to a showdown, the ITV companies relented, though only at the last minute. This was virtually inevitable once the boards were confronted with evidence that so many of their largest shareholders were opposed to the original proposed boardroom structure. The board of Granada was the first to blink, deciding that the proposals could not go through as originally planned. Their decision was seen as a something of a betrayal at Carlton, which then reluctantly followed suit. The Carlton chairman, Michael Green, was the one who departed, leaving Charles Allen of Granada in place as the chief executive of the newly merged company. Some time later, Sir Peter Burt, the former governor of Bank of Scotland, and a man with a reputation for toughness, accepted the job of ITV chairman and in due course confirmed the appointment of Allen as chief executive. Bolton, who had earlier touted another name as a possible chairman, says he was happy with the choice and remains a shareholder in the new ITV company.

In hindsight, could the whole messy ITV saga have been avoided with more careful handling on all sides? Given the high stakes involved for those on the company side, arguably not. Bolton's view throughout was that the row would best have been dealt with quietly behind closed doors, as happens, he claims, in a good many other corporate governance cases that never reach the public eye. The ITV saga is interesting mainly because it points to the growing influence that institutional shareholders as a group are now starting to exert on the behaviour of quoted companies, something which they have been criticised for not doing in the past. In an interview with Real IR magazine in 2004, Bolton said that Fidelity typically intervenes in some 50 cases a year, of which only a fraction are likely to be reported. While it remains the job of company boards to decide how businesses should be run, he says that Fidelity expects to be consulted about big strategic decisions, such as M&A proposals, or disposals of business, that are likely to rebound on the value of the company's shares.*

The irony is that if whoever leaked the original story intended to try and spike Bolton's guns, it probably had the reverse effect: once challenged by the companies to prove his views were widely shared, Fidelity had no option but to join forces with other leading shareholders and insist on a change. In the process, although he found the intense media coverage uncomfortable, and the 'quiet assassin' tag distressing, the episode has served to underline

---

* The Appendix, page 160, has a full version of the interview. See also page 70.

how much influence Bolton now enjoys in the City. "Because his manner is so quiet", says his colleague Simon Fraser, "it is easy for those who don't know Anthony well to underestimate the strength of his feelings. The non-executive directors of the ITV companies may genuinely not have appreciated initially quite how serious his reservations about the proposed management of the merged company were." When it came to a showdown, however, the fact that Bolton was prepared to put his hard-earned reputation on the line over the issue was clearly an important, and maybe even the decisive, factor in persuading Fidelity to press the issue, and the boards of the two companies to back down. The outcome is one more indication of how far the shy and thoughtful 29-year-old recruit of 1979 with a flair for picking stocks has travelled in the ensuing 25 years.

Daring to be different

My 25 years as a contrarian investor
by Anthony Bolton

How it all began

The year that Margaret Thatcher was first elected Prime Minister in the UK, 1979, was one of the key years in my life. Looking back, I realise that I did what I think stress consultants advise most strongly against – which is getting married, moving house and moving jobs all in a relatively short period of time. I got married in February 1979, having moved house a few weeks before, and then changed job to join Fidelity in December. I had met my wife Sarah while we both worked at Schlesinger Investment Management, a South African owned investment company which also had interests in banking and property. She was an assistant to one of the investment directors and I was, at first, an investment assistant and later a fund manager. In the summer of that year one of the two managing directors, Richard Timberlake, left Schlesingers to start a new fund management business for Fidelity in the UK. He let it be known that he was looking for two investment managers to join his nascent organisation.

I hesitated whether to contact him as I was told he had agreed not to try and actively recruit his ex-colleagues for a period of time. I also knew little or nothing about Fidelity. Two things changed my mind. The first was making contact with a personal friend who worked as an investment manager at M&G, the company that had introduced the first unit trust in England back in the 1930s. He told me that Fidelity was "the best US manager in the business". The second was my wife Sarah, who could see the potential and significance of the new company, and persuaded me to give Richard Timberlake a call. I was then aged 29, rather shy and somewhat hesitant about ringing up. "What have you got to lose?" she repeatedly asked me, until I made the call. It turned out to be one of the most important calls that I have ever made.

After a meeting with Richard, he asked me to have an interview with Bill Byrnes. Bill had worked at Fidelity's headquarters in Boston for many years and was very close to Ned Johnson, who was the President of Fidelity as well as the son of the company's founder. If Ned Johnson is entitled to the credit for Fidelity's phenomenal success in the US in the 1980s and 1990s, then Bill Byrnes is the man who deserves the credit for starting Fidelity's international business. This was at a time when most US investment businesses were purely focused on their domestic market in North America.

Youthful recruit: Fidelity's youngest UK director

As one of the market leaders in the US mutual fund business, Fidelity was well ahead of the times in seeing the potential for taking its investment business into the global market. I remember that the news was deemed sufficiently important by the Financial Times to be given front page treatment, though I don't think many other papers took much notice.

I went for my interview with Bill with some trepidation. I had after all only run money for a year or two at Schlesingers. I was hardly the most experienced fund manager in the UK. The last question I was asked was:

"Well Anthony, do you think you can run money successfully at Fidelity and beat the competition?" I can't remember my answer, but something must have persuaded him I could do it because shortly afterwards I was offered the job. Bill is one of the most charming Americans one can meet and a great Anglophile. He has been a constant source of encouragement to me over the years. He still calls into our London office once or twice a year.

So it was that I joined Fidelity on 17th December 1979, the day that the company launched its first four unit trusts for British investors. As well as my fund, the Fidelity Special Situations Trust, there was an American Trust (not surprisingly, given Fidelity's parentage), a Fixed Interest Trust and a Growth and Income Trust run by the other investment manager that Richard recruited. His name was James Wellings. He had previously worked for a stockbroker and he ran money in a very different style to mine. He bought low risk, higher yielding shares with a very quantitative approach that involved regularly taking profits on companies that had outperformed the stock market as a whole.

We shared an office for the first few years in Fidelity's then City office in Queen Street. James was a lovely individual, very much of the old school, a traditionalist, as I suppose I am. We got on very well. The only exception was for a couple of weeks in the early months we were together. When I was interviewed by Richard Timberlake, I had made it a condition of joining that I wanted to be a director; one of my personal ambitions was to become a director before I was thirty years old. James hadn't asked for the same condition and, although he was also made a director later, my appointment predated his by a few months. Being equally ambitious, he was very upset that I had beaten him to the post. This made sharing a small office awkward for a while, but he soon forgot about it and thereafter we got on brilliantly.[1]

The Fidelity experience

When I first joined Fidelity, I think that there were about twelve of us in the Queen Street office, consisting of Richard Timberlake's initial team, plus three or four people whom Fidelity already had in London to help run their offshore funds. Several of these funds, based in Bermuda, had been going for some years before the launch of the UK unit trust company in 1979. They were

---

[1] James left Fidelity some time later to pursue other interests.

Fidelity's first offerings to international investors. It seems amazing now that 25 years later Fidelity employs more than 3,210 people (as of the 31st March 2004) in the UK. This includes an investment team with 34 portfolio managers and 54 analysts, based in our office at 25 Cannon Street. This office, which we designed, built and own ourselves, looks out over St Paul's Cathedral. It is the fourth office Fidelity has had in the City. A growing investment management business is generally short of office space and managing one's property needs is an important but difficult administrative task.

I am often asked how I have stuck it out for 25 years at the same company and what it is that has kept me at Fidelity. Obviously there are a number of factors. The first has been the excitement and satisfaction of having been part of the team that has built up what in my view is the number one investment management institution in the UK. I have been lucky to have been intimately involved in setting up and shaping the investment team. Secondly, it has given me the opportunity to work with some of the brightest, most talented and nicest people in the business. This last attribute is particularly important to me. I have had a number of approaches over the years to join other companies, although the headhunters have stopped ringing me in recent years as they all know it's a waste of time trying to persuade me to move.

I remember one approach in the 1980s from what was then one of the most successful global hedge fund businesses of the time. This was a second attempt as I had met the proprietor a few years earlier. This time I met the head of international investment and I must say that I thought he was a particularly unpleasant person. He ended our meeting by saying something along the lines that he couldn't understand why British people didn't think getting rich was the most important aim in life and were motivated by other things besides money.

The great thing about Fidelity is that we have a superb group of people with a mutual shared interest: every senior person has either been involved in running money personally or, if they haven't, knows that doing this well is the one activity that guides everything else that Fidelity does. The quality of the people has been the key to keeping me here and the special environment this creates is also, I think, why we have been able to retain so many of our good investment personnel. Obviously reward and incentives are very important as well but they are not everything. I also think it is a big advantage working for a privately owned business in which it is possible to make decisions for the long term. One investment manager at a competitor firm whom I met told me that they had been through three reorganisations of their investment management side in the last four years. This was the result of other investment organisations being brought into the group by acquisition; each reorganisation involved a number of people leaving and the chief investment officer changing. Fidelity's growth has all been organic and it's been our key philosophy to build our own team rather than go out and buy other firms. I am convinced that this is the best way to motivate and keep key staff. It's interesting – and probably no coincidence – that another of the largest and most successful global investment businesses, Capital Research, is also privately owned and has grown organically.

The Special Situations fund

Why did I start a Special Situations Trust and what does this term really mean? Richard Timberlake knew at the outset that he wanted me to start a fund that was primarily focused on capital growth, to complement the more defensive qualities of the Growth and Income Trust. As one of the funds I had helped to run at Schlesingers was the Schlesinger Special Situations Trust, and as it was also the fund I enjoyed managing the most, it was natural for me to suggest to Richard that this is what we should launch. He agreed, and so the fund was born. If you had told me then that the fund would one day grow to more than £4 billion in assets, and become the best performing unit trust of the next 25 years, I would have been amazed. We started in a much more modest way, with the simple idea of seeing how well we could do and taking it from there.

The first definition of what constitutes a 'special situation' was set out in the prospectus of the unit trust when it was launched. Over the years I have refined and modified the way I describe my approach, but the basic concept – searching for capital growth opportunities in an aggressive and contrarian way – remains exactly the same as at the outset. In the prospectus for Fidelity Special Values Plc, the investment trust that I also run on the same lines as the unit trust, but launched a few years later, the description runs as follows:

"The Manager regards as a 'Special Situation' a company attractively valued in relation to net assets, dividend yield or future earnings per share, but which, in its view, has additionally some other specific features that could have a positive influence on its share price." The types of companies which may fall within the definition of 'special situation', it went on, include:

- Companies with recovery potential
- Companies with strong growth potential
- Companies with assets whose value has not generally been recognised
- Companies with a special product which has a particular market niche and therefore good earnings potential
- Companies which are possible takeover candidates
- Companies subject to restructuring and/or changes in management
- Companies which are not widely researched by the brokerage community

The fund manager, we said, "is likely to concentrate on companies which it considers to be out of favour with investors or undervalued in relation to generally accepted valuation measures, but where it believes investor sentiment is likely to improve in the medium term". That would lead us to focus on shares in companies outside the market leaders. We would adopt a 'bottom-up' stockpicking approach, selecting investments "primarily on the basis of specific criteria relevant to the company in question and not on the basis of general macro-economic considerations". Noting the importance of doing our own research, we added: "As well as the analysis of the company's financial position and their relative valuations, the manager meets the management of a significant number of such companies. It aims thereby to build an information advantage which previous experience has indicated can be utilised to exploit the market inefficiencies and hidden values in under-researched companies. After investment in a company, the manager will follow it closely and, generally, maintain contact with the management in order to identify at an early stage any change in its situation or prospects."

This still very well encapsulates my approach. It is important that the definition of what constitutes a special situation has always been pretty wide, which means that many different types of situation can be included. If your objective is the aggressive pursuit of capital growth, as mine has always been, it makes no sense to exclude potential moneymaking opportunities by being too restrictive about what kind of shares you can buy. Another key phrase in the prospectus definition is "…..which it considers to be out of favour with investors or undervalued". My investment style has always been at heart a 'value' approach.

Of the two most important investment styles – growth and value – why did I choose value? I think there are several reasons. Firstly, I have always liked reading books on investment that are written about, or by, the great investment gurus. In my opinion the weight of the evidence of these supports the idea that value is more likely than growth to deliver superior returns over the long term. This does not mean that I dismiss growth as a valid way to produce above average returns. It is merely that over the long term the odds are slightly more in one's favour with a value approach. Another factor that influenced me at the beginning was the fact that one of the most popular unit trusts at the time was the M&G Recovery Fund. It was run with a broadly value style that involved buying companies that had done poorly. I very much identified with its policy of buying out of favour companies.

Finally, I believe that investment managers should find a style and mode of operation that works for them personally and then stick to that style. For some reason I have always felt happier going against the crowd and generally feel uncomfortable doing what everyone else is doing. So many pressures in the investment business encourage one to do the opposite and go with the crowd. Unless you are temperamentally happy with acting on your own, this approach is unlikely to do you much good. People have asked me if my general approach to life is also contrarian, but I don't think it is. Generally in my personal life I will follow what I like, which sometimes may be fashionable and sometimes not. What I have found is that my contrarian stock market style is particularly helpful at market turning points when the natural tendency is often to do completely the wrong thing. Experience, I believe, counts for a great deal in investment. As Mark Twain said, "History never repeats itself but it sometimes rhymes." I think these eight words should be burned into every fund manager's desk.

Ignoring the benchmark

John Maynard Keynes, who was a very successful investor as well as an outstandingly original economist, said in regard to the stock market that picking shares was like a beauty contest where "it is important to choose not who you think is the prettiest girl, but who the judges will think is the prettiest girl". Another way to put this, to borrow a phrase from Ben Graham, is that the stock market is more of a voting machine than a weighing machine, at least in the short term. I have always started my search amongst the stocks that investors don't think are the prettiest, so that if they change – and I'm really using my skills to find ones that have the factors that might lead to a change – there will be lots of new buyers for the shares as they become more attractive. (In life, as opposed to the stock market, however, I recommend you pick the girl that you think is the prettiest. I certainly did.)

One of the most important features of the Fidelity Special Situations Fund, which flows directly from my contrarian philosophy, is that I have always run it on an unbenchmarked basis. That is to say, I pay little attention to how what I own compares with the makeup of the FTSE All-Share Index. The All-Share Index is the measure, or benchmark, against which my performance is judged: and the objective of the fund is to do better than the index. But, unlike many fund managers with the same objective, I do not spend time worrying whether I have say 10% in oil company shares at a time when the index has 15%, or whether I do or do not own the biggest component companies in the index.

This indifference to the benchmark's weightings by definition means that over time my fund produces more 'lumpy' returns than the market averages. I have inevitably had bad patches during my 25 years in charge of the Special Situations fund. However, at the heart of my approach is the view encapsulated by Warren Buffett when he said that he and his partner Charlie Munger "would much rather earn a lumpy 15% [per annum] over time than a smooth 12%". My objective is to provide the highest average annual return that I can in the long term, even though this return will fluctuate more in the short term. It is the opposite of a benchmarked fund which attempts to provide a modest amount of relative performance on a consistent quarter by quarter basis, building up over time to a smoother, but lower, long term return.

In the early days of Fidelity I also ran some money for pension fund clients such as Tate & Lyle and Rank Xerox. However, my heart has always been primarily on the unit trust side. One of the reasons is the very wide freedom that one has to manage a unit trust in comparison to a pension fund, where there is the constant burden of trustees questioning your actions after the event. In those days, it seemed to me, pension fund trustees always wanted to spend the most time talking about the investment decisions that hadn't gone right, or at least had not gone right at the moment of reporting.

Yet investment is an odds game. No-one gets it right all the time; we are all trying to make fewer mistakes than our competitors. In fact, the key to success in this business is as much to avoid losers as it is to pick winners. On the other hand, running money with a style that is so defensive that it avoids all losers is also, I believe, counterproductive to superior returns. Having a calm temperament is another very important factor. One should learn from one's losers but not get too upset about them. Conversely it is unwise to overcelebrate the winners; overconfidence can be just as bad. It is always worth remembering that some of your best performing stocks could have been picked just as easily with a pin!

In the mid 1980s I took on the added responsibility of managing Fidelity's European Trust when this was launched. Europe particularly interested me as, from an investment point of view, the markets were very underdeveloped compared to the UK and therefore the opportunities for finding mispriced shares were abundant. It was a very rewarding environment for a stockpicker such as myself. As our team grew, I was able to give up my institutional accounts to focus solely on these two funds. In 1990 I also took on management of our Luxembourg-based fund Fidelity Funds – European Growth which subsequently became Fidelity International's largest fund. It started as a fund that invested only in continental Europe, with no UK exposure, but later became a Pan-European Fund that included UK shares as well.

In the early 1990s we launched two closed-end investment trusts, Fidelity European Values Plc in 1991 and Fidelity Special Values in 1994. Both of these I ran with similar portfolios to their sister unit trusts. The investment trusts provide investors with alternative ways to invest in my stockpicking abilities and can also, unlike the unit trusts, use gearing (borrowing) to enhance returns. At times when the investment trusts sell at a significant discount to their net asset value, they can be particularly attractive alternatives to the open-ended funds.

In the last couple of years I have given up my European funds to focus on just Special Situations Fund and Special Values Plc, which together (as of mid 2004) have assets of about £4bn. Running four funds, including Fidelity's three largest ones, had become extremely demanding, involving monitoring 400 individual shareholdings and doing three or more company meetings every day; I had come to a stage in my life when I wanted to cut down my responsibilities. This effectively meant giving up either the UK or continental Europe, and I decided to do the latter and return to where I had started.

Drama in the markets

During the last 25 years four events particularly stick in my mind. They are the stock market crash of 1987, the invasion of Kuwait in 1991, the technology bubble in 1999/2000 and the terrorist attack on New York in September 2001, now commonly known as 9/11. About a week before the 1987 crash, our youngest child Ben was born at Queen Charlotte's Hospital in London. To be near my wife Sarah, I was staying with my parents who lived in Holland Park in London rather than our home in Hampshire where my mother-in-law was looking after our elder two children, Emma and Oliver. On the Thursday night, there was the great storm which wrought havoc across Southern England. Even in London, I found it hard to sleep, being kept awake by the wind.

The next day when I made my way to work by tube from Holland Park station, the streets were covered with a thick, green carpet of leaves and small branches from the trees along Holland Park Avenue, creating a rather surreal effect. It had been our intention to return to our home in the country that weekend when Sarah and Ben came out of hospital, but the storm put a stop to that. There was no electricity at our house and a tree had fallen on my car, making it a write off. Sensibly my mother-in-law had decided to take our two elder children, our mother's help and our golden retriever 'Kingston' back to her home in Devon, which was much less badly affected. So Sarah and Ben came to join me at my parents' house, and that is where we were the following Monday when the crash hit Wall Street. I felt very disorientated, firstly not being at home as I expected, and then having to live through the most extraordinary few days in the stock market that I have ever experienced.

Professional opinion after the crash was polarised. I remember one experienced investment manager telling me: "If the world's largest market can fall by more than 22% in a day, investing will never be the same again." There were plenty of commentators who predicted that the crash would bring about a huge recession, or even a depression. I remember going to a lunch with the Australian entrepreneur, Alan Bond, who was definitely in this pessimistic camp. Whether it was my optimistic nature, or my contrarian investment approach, I didn't see it that way. I remember arguing that markets would recover and the crash had therefore created a significant buying opportunity. I even sent around a note internally at Fidelity to this effect, which is something that I have not done very often. At the heart of my argument was the feeling that it was very unlikely that the scale of the stockmarket fall would be matched by a similar deterioration in the economy.

I had redemptions to deal with in my funds, with several investors deciding to sell their units in the fund in the wake of the market crash. As a result I had to sell shares that the fund owned in order to meet the redemptions. In times of panic such as the 1987 crash, I find it helpful to concentrate my portfolio. I focus in on the stocks I like the most and force myself to identify those about which I have the strongest convictions. I have found I have a tendency to allow the number of holdings in the fund to rise as a bull market progresses. Market downturns are therefore also a good opportunity to weed out some of the smaller holdings that have accumulated in the portfolio.

Fortunately, by the end of 1987, despite the dramatic falls in the market during the month of October, I still ended the year with the fund up 28.0%, with the market up 7.3%. However, just before the crash the fund was up an exceptional 97.4% since the start of the year, in a period when the market had risen 45.6%. I guess I should have seen the magnitude of these moves as a warning sign, but at least overall my fund was not too badly affected.

For Fidelity International as a business, the crash had much deeper effects. In the years leading up to it we had been through a phase of strong growth and staff numbers had risen rapidly. We had some management meetings in Paris during November 1987 to coincide with the launch of our French business (in retrospect, it was not the most auspicious timing for a launch).

At work today: the bowler hat is now redundant

At these meetings, our Chief Executive showed some graphs on the performance of Fidelity's business. These showed a worrying picture of a rising expense line meeting a falling revenue line. As a result we had to carry out a major restructuring of the business over the next year or so, including some layoffs. There is an unwritten rule at Fidelity that during downturns the investment team should be excluded from any redundancies. By protecting the lifeblood of the business, which is its investment expertise, we were able to maintain intact the team which was subsequently responsible for Fidelity's success in the 1990s.

At the time of the invasion of Kuwait three years later, I was on holiday in Portugal. For several summers in a row we had rented houses on the Algarve for two weeks in August. In the days before mobile phones, I always insisted on any house we rented having a telephone in case I needed to make contact with the office. Having been promised that our villa outside Albufeira had a phone, when we got there we found it, of course, out of order! Every day for a week I contacted both the villa company and the telephone exchange to try and get it repaired, but with no effect. After the invasion of Kuwait, I ended up having to drive into Albufeira at least once every day to hear what the redemptions were and to give instructions regarding which securities to sell. Although I delegate trading to one of our traders who works with me on my purchases and sales, I will hardly ever delegate the decision of what to buy and sell (unless there is an emergency and I can't be contacted). Over the years, I have found it pretty rare that I have had to spend a lot of a holiday on the telephone to the office – but 1991 was the exception.

The internet bubble

The technology bubble in 1999-2000 was one of the most extraordinary periods in the stock market that I have witnessed. I am often asked how I can justify being a picker of stocks in a period when the investment markets have become so professional. They say things like: "Isn't the market efficient and overresearched? Haven't most of the investment anomalies already been exploited?" All I need to do in reply is point to this period, which presented some of the biggest opportunities in the shares of 'old economy' companies that I have ever experienced. How did it ever come about? Well at its heart must be the herd-like nature of most investment institutions, the intellectual challenge of a new paradigm ("the internet will change everything") and the cult at the time of momentum investing.

My general impression is that the market today frequently fails to see the wood for the trees; it's so busy arbitraging out the small inefficiencies between the trees, it misses that the wood itself is inefficiently priced. For example, I remember great debate at the time about which of Logica or Sage was the more attractive IT stock to own in the Information Technology sector. The answer was they were both wildly overvalued. I gave an internal talk in 2000 to our portfolio managers and analysts about bubbles – their nature, historical examples and how they burst. There were a few events that really drove it home to me that we were in cloud-cuckoo land.

One was the valuations of many companies in the TMT sectors. A software company called Kewill Systems particularly sticks in my mind. I had followed Kewill since its IPO (initial public offering) in the mid 1980s and also visited the original head office in Walton-on-Thames in the early days. The company was involved in the exciting areas of supply chain & e-commerce software. Between June 1999 and March 2000, its market capitalisation rose more than ten times to over £2 billion, at which point the shares traded at more than 60 times its sales. Since then the share price has fallen from £31 to 73p, having been as low as 7.5p at one stage in 2002. What was surprising was that this pattern of excess valuation was repeated again and again: I even recall one Swiss software company that was called Fantastic Corporation – sadly it was fantastic for a short while only!

A second, rather different indicator was the fate of Tony Dye at PFDM, one of the City's largest pension fund management firms. Tony Dye must be considered as one of the leading proponents in London of value investing. He and PDFM parted company in February 2000, two weeks before the NASDAQ index peaked on 10th March. At the same time PDFM announced that it was reviewing whether it should stick with its longstanding value style of investment. To any contrarian, this was a classic signal that the market was approaching a turning point, as of course it proved to be.

Lastly there was an event that particularly sticks in my memory. A long-standing corporate finance contact of mine telephoned me with a proposition. He was floating an internet incubator fund via a placing of shares. [Incubator funds were a popular fad of the time, designed to invest in a range of start-up internet companies and in theory help them grow]. I think he had been allowed to approach eight institutions. The conversation went something like this: "Hello Anthony, I want to tell you about a very interesting new company I am listing." "Great," I said "when can we meet the management?" "I'm afraid we are doing it on an accelerated basis and that won't be possible. In fact, I need to know your interest by this evening. Anthony, you should know that every institution that I have contacted so far not only wants shares, but says they would be happy to take many more than we are offering them."

We then went through the figures on the company. The fund owned a mixture of listed and unlisted companies related to the internet. I worked out that if one valued the listed investments at market prices, one was paying five or six times book value for the unlisted ones – a very, very high valuation in my opinion. "Thanks", I said "it's not for us.", "I beg your pardon, Anthony", he replied. "Thanks, but it's not for us", I repeated. "But Anthony," came the reply "you'll be the only institution to have turned this down." "Fidelity is happy to let this one pass", I replied. This was only a few weeks from the top of the TMT bubble and the writing was clearly on the wall. I didn't follow what happened to this company in the end, but I very much doubt that it survived. The incredulity of my corporate finance contact tells its own story about what happens during bubbles of this kind.

On the day of 9/11, I was having lunch with a contact who runs a small specialist broking firm. He is an expert on general (i.e. non-life) insurance. We talked mainly about the insurance industry over lunch and by the end he had convinced me, or we had convinced each other, that the outlook appeared pretty good. I suppose it was ironic that just as we were drinking our coffee, the worst insurance event in recorded history should be taking place on the other side of the Atlantic. I know it may sound callous, but my experience suggested that over the months following that terrible event (and I can't think of a more horrendous one) a very important buying opportunity would occur in the companies that had been worst affected by the fallout from the terrorist attack. I later significantly increased my holdings in insurance, hotel and travel related companies, and made some good returns as the shares recovered. In the investment business one has to be hard-nosed at times, unfortunately, but it is part of what being a contrarian involves.

The changing investment scene

From its earliest days, Fidelity's investment approach has been based on conducting its own research, using in-house analysts and having regular meetings with the companies it invests in. This was an approach with which I readily identified. My first job in 1971 was in the investment department of Keyser Ullmann, a small merchant bank which mainly managed investment trusts, including one called the Throgmorton Trust. Its focus was on smaller companies (a bias that I have kept ever since) and doing one's own research (though in those days that nearly always meant visiting the companies at their own offices; few companies came to the City and when they did, it wasn't to visit investors). The analyst team at Keyser Ullman included, as well as fundamental analysts, one technical analyst. Since then I have always used charts as an input into my approach – something that I found was also Fidelity's philosophy. My background was therefore well suited to Fidelity, which may be something that Bill Byrnes had spotted.

In the early days the investment department was very small and it was only in the mid 1980s that we started to build up our own team of in-house analysts. We did some individual company meetings in those days, but it was more normal to attend group meetings at broker offices, where a number of institutions met with the management of a company at the same time. I do remember a meeting that James Wellings and I had in the early years with a company in our office at Queen Street. I can't remember the name of the company, but I do remember the name of its Chief Executive, which was Ron Shuck. Later he was involved in a major fraud case.

From the mid 1980s onwards, more and more of the meetings were one-to-one meetings with companies in our own offices. From the late 1980s I started to keep my notes of meetings in hard backed notebooks which I keep in my office. I have a different set of books for each European country. I am now up to my 42nd book of notes on UK company meetings. These notes are invaluable when I re-meet companies. When I also ran the European funds, I used to do three or four company meetings a day. I now do one or two a day on average. My record, I think, is six company meetings in one day, which I don't recommend as one is rushing from one to the next and one feels pretty washed out at the end of the day.

Our meetings are normally with the Chief Executive (CEO) and/or the Finance Director. In bigger companies it may be just with an investor relations officer. Meetings normally last one to one and a half hours and we like to meet or have contact with companies at least once a quarter if we have significant holdings. We also use conference calls where we know the company well. The meetings are run by the appropriate analyst, not by the fund managers. Each of our analysts specialise in different industries and produce an agenda and financial model before each meeting. The fund managers also chip in with questions from time to time.

The way we run our meetings has not changed significantly over time. One thing I definitely notice, however, is that while I used to be younger than most of the chief executives, today the opposite is definitely the case. At the end of a company meeting there is often a debriefing session where the investment managers discuss the key conclusions and cross-examine the analyst on the assumptions in their financial models.

I remember going to a dinner in the early 1990s that had been arranged by a broker where several senior representatives of companies and institutional investors were present. One of the subjects discussed was what sort of contact institutions want with companies. I explained our approach and said I thought it was going to become the norm for many larger institutions. I remember one of the chief executives taking issue with me. He said, "how am I going to have any time to run my company if I'm going to have to spend a lot of my time with shareholders and prospective shareholders?" I would estimate that today investor relations activities are something that most CEOs spend a significant amount of their time on. Often ones that have historically done less of this (Shell and M&S are two examples that come to mind) have suffered as a result of their introspective culture.

I believe Fidelity's approach of in-house analysts and one-to-one company meetings has become the blueprint for many of our competitors. What was quite unusual in the early 1990s is standard practise today. It's been good to have been ahead of the crowd, but nothing stands still. One of the things I spend time thinking about today is how we can stay ahead. If we only do what everyone else is doing, it will become harder to outperform even if we are doing it on a scale and with more resources that most of our competitors. One area where we think we remain ahead is in the quality and depth of our global research, using information gleaned in one country or region to help make investments in another. Very few institutions can match our global resources.

Broking and research

Another area which has changed dramatically over the 25 years is the brokerage community. As well as using the best internal research one can, I have always been a proponent of using the best outside research to complement it. With one's own research, one needs to know whether the conclusions differ from the consensus view, which itself is often made by the key analysts at the different stockbrokers who follow a particular company.

Because of Big Bang and the spate of takeovers which followed deregulation of the stock market in 1986, most stockbrokers have changed hands (some several times) during the last 25 years.

Among the larger broking firms, the new approach of combining proprietary trading with investment banking and research means that the business model has been completely transformed from the old partnership structures that existed when I started out. Has the quality of output from broking houses changed, and do I share the view that most of the output from brokers today has little value? I don't agree with that. The nature of what analysts are able to put in writing has certainly changed. It is also true that in many cases broking research is being increasingly used for investment banking purposes. Nevertheless I believe that if you know how to use research and which analysts to talk to, it can still be very valuable. This is particularly true of those nuances an analyst may have that cannot easily be explained in writing.

In the early years the broker we were closest to was Rowe & Pitman (long ago amalgamated into what is now UBS Investment Bank). They had helped Fidelity launch its offshore funds. They gave me some excellent advice at the time. I also remember a visit from two executives at Goldman Sachs. They had no real research or involvement in the UK stock market at the time, but said if they could assist with anything to do with the US market or elsewhere, they would be only too delighted to help. (Fidelity in the US was at the time one of their biggest clients.) I did in due course find some areas where they were of help.

The secret of picking stocks

In general, my approach to picking stocks has always been based on a wide range of inputs. My philosophy is that the more ideas that find their way to me, the better. The way I like to put it is that I want a wide 'net'. The more that comes in, whether from inside Fidelity, or from smaller broking houses, industry specialists or the big integrated investment banks, the greater my chances of finding a gem. As my former colleague Peter Lynch once put it: "If you turn over ten stones, you might find one attractive investment idea but if you turn over 100 stones, you might find ten." Running large funds one needs lots of ideas. Even with a big in-house team we can't cover, or be the expert, on everything.

Trying to explain what makes me buy one stock and not another is surprisingly difficult, even after all these years. What is true is that before I buy a company I like to have considered a number of factors. First, wherever possible, I like to have met the management. The meeting will do several key things: help me get a view of the people and the strategy; help me understand the quality of the businesses and the main variables which influence their financial performance (some of these may be in management's control, others, such as currency sensitivity, largely not). I am a great believer that businesses are not created equal – some have much better franchises than others and other things being equal, I like those with the better franchises.

The meeting will also allow us to build a financial model of the company as accurate as any done by third parties. I will then want to look at a number of valuation metrics. I am always keen to look at a range of valuation measures and not focus too much on just one measure. The key ones I look at will be P/E (price-earnings) ratios, the ratio of enterprise value to gross cash flow, free cashflow ratios (I like companies that generate free cashflow) and cash flow return on capital relative to invested capital. I will also look at how the company is valued against its industry peer group on a country, region and global basis.

I will then want to look at some balance sheet ratios to see how strong the balance sheet is; one vital lesson I have learnt over the years is that when things go wrong, the companies I have lost most money on are those with weak balance sheets. I will also consider the list of shareholders and whether there is a possible 'corporate angle' to the stock. I will also look at the company from a corporate governance point of view, whether there has been director buying or selling and what technical analysts are saying about the shares. I will also consider whether the shares are over or under owned by institutional investors, whether there has been net buying or selling and what the key broker analysts who cover the shares views are.

Finally, I will consider whether there is something about the share that investors are not focused on today, but which could re-excite interest in the future. This list is not exclusive and there can also be other factors I will consider on top of these. I can't understate the importance in my approach of looking at a wide range of factors before I decide to buy the shares of a company. I observe that other investors often want to use a 'shorthand'

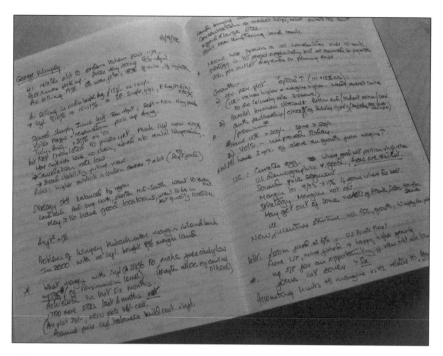

All meetings with companies are noted and filed away.

approach to investment, just using one input as their buying or selling criterion. An extreme example of this would be buying shares on a tip, or merely looking at a share price chart in isolation. The fact that many less experienced investors seem to want an easy or (dare I say?) lazy approach to stock selection does, I believe, help to throw up opportunities for professional investors like myself, who will always be looking more deeply at an amalgam of buy and sell considerations.

The size of the fund and its performance

An important change that I have had to adjust to over the years has been learning how to run a large fund instead of a small one. Special Situations has been more than £1 billion in size for more than five years, which makes it one of the biggest funds in the UK. Looking back at the early reports to unitholders, I see a fund which was valued at a mere few million pounds. In those reports I reported that: "A large number of ideas are sifted by the Investment Manager to arrive at a concentrated portfolio of about 30-40 shares." Over the years, to cope with the large volumes of money that have flowed into the fund, I have had to increase both the number of holdings and increase the fund's exposure to larger companies. Today I have about 200 holdings in the fund, which is five to six times the number in those early years.

Working for an organisation that already had experience of running very large funds has been a help in this regard. Fidelity Magellan, the fund which made Peter Lynch's name and grew rapidly on the back of his success, was for some time the largest mutual fund in America. I had a lunch meeting in Boston in the late 1980s with both Peter and Bruce Johnson, an equally successful, though less well known, Fidelity manager who ran the firm's largest income funds. They gave me a lot of advice. One thing in particular I remember. They told me to make sure that, however big the fund became, I was still spending enough time on 'offensive' investment.

What they meant by this was that when you run a large fund with a lot of holdings, you can, as an investment manager, end up spending most of your time keeping tabs on the current holdings ('defensive' investing) rather than going out to look for new ideas. They recommended using the in-house team of analysts to help with the defensive part of the fund's work, that is monitoring results, company announcements and industry developments in existing holdings, in order to free up more time to do the hunting for new ideas. This has been my approach ever since.

The other thing I have done is to ask myself repeatedly what are the things that a large fund can do which a small fund cannot. Two in particular I have found to be important. One is buying holdings that might have a 'corporate' value at some stage in the future, owing to their size as a percentage of the company's issued share capital; and the second is becoming more active in engaging with management where a company is not doing well and one has views on how its plight might be improved.

On the first, I have always been interested in stocks with a 'corporate angle' – in other words, companies where there is the prospect of a change of ownership or control – and it is one of the main categories of company that I buy. A good example of one of these was the holding that Fidelity had in the French bank Credit Lyonnais. When Credit Lyonnais was privatised by the French State, it was given a two-stage scheme of protection in order to stop it from being taken over against its wishes. For the first two years this protection was pretty tight but it relaxed somewhat in the subsequent two years. During the first two years, I built up a sizeable holding. Fidelity became one of the biggest institutional shareholders in the bank.

I thought that the bank's shares were an interesting investment anyway, but I also thought that a takeover battle was likely to develop at some stage down the road. This was in fact what happened, with two other French banks competing at one stage to buy it. We were able to sell our stake in Credit Lyonnais to Credit Agricole at a decent premium to the market price. This illustrated my view that, in certain circumstances, a large shareholding could have a value in a takeover that is greater than the market value. Being a large shareholder can also be decisive in determining whether a takeover bid for a company happens at all.

The corporate governance front

On the corporate governance front, getting involved to help bring about change in a company's management can produce both good and bad news. My involvement in the affairs of ITV in the summer of 2003 gave me a much higher profile in the media than I have had before, and certainly more publicity than I would have liked. At the heart of what we do at Fidelity whenever we get involved in a change of management or strategy at a company is the simple objective of improving the value of our investments in the future. There are two aspects to this. The first is helping to raise standards in general across corporate Europe. The second is 'intervention' in a single company for specific reasons.

Most of the work we do on the corporate governance front is in private, directly with companies rather than in the public eye. The ITV case was very rare in that our agenda for a change of chairman became public through a leak to the media (not at our instigation, I hasten to add). It is also rare for our activity to be associated with a single individual at Fidelity, as happened to me in the ITV story: in nearly all cases, we are putting pressure for changes in conjunction with other large investors. In general, the investments we focus on are underperforming companies where, if we can influence a beneficial change in direction, such action gives us an alternative to selling the shares, something that is naturally harder do effectively the bigger your fund becomes. My funds have often been the largest single Fidelity holding

Corporate governance: "acting quietly behind the scenes is very much the way we prefer to operate".

in companies where we have 'intervened'. In total Fidelity 'intervened' in about fifty UK and European companies in 2003, though few of these ever made the press or attracted any public attention. Acting quietly behind the scenes is very much the way we prefer to operate.

As the size of the fund increases, so the manager's flexibility and room for manoeuvre reduces. Given the average size of my holdings (now £10 million is normally a minimum sized holding), it is difficult for me today to make wholesale changes to the portfolio in a short space of time. In any case making dramatic quickfire changes to my portfolio has never been my style. Nor is it is well suited to running a large fund. My preferred approach is an incremental one. I often make small changes to the size of my holding in an individual stock as my conviction either increases or decreases over time. This could be the result of a company meeting, a piece of news, advice from our analyst, or some piece of technical analysis. Normally my initial size of holding is 25 basis points (0.25% of the funds assets) and I will increase from there depending on my conviction and the stock's marketability.

At other times I have made changes to the portfolio on the basis of broader investment considerations, for example increasing the number of holdings in companies which are likely to benefit from increased corporate spending, as opposed to those which are more exposed to consumer spending (as I did in the second half of 2003). This type of change occurs at the margin. As it normally takes a number of days to build or reduce a holding, unless a large block of shares is available or wanted in the market, I find that I always have more ideas than I need. I know I will not be able to consummate all of them. Sometimes there may not be stock available. Alternatively the price may rush away, rising too fast for me to build the position I want at the right price.

Good and bad performance

As a fund manager, it goes without saying that you are always looking to balance the potential returns against the risk of loss. I am often asked "when historically have you done poorly?" In the last 25 years there have been seven years in which I have underperformed the FTSE All-Share Index as, is shown in the chart opposite.

My times of underperformance have generally coincided either with UK recessions (the early 1980s and the early 1990s) or with 'momentum' markets (the mid 1980s and late 1990s). Recessions tend to be difficult periods for medium and smaller companies and in 'momentum' markets, the biggest companies (an area in which I have always been structurally underweight) do best. One might have expected 1999, the last year of the great momentum markets of the later 1990s, to have been a worse year than it was for me, but I was helped by an exceptional number of takeovers that year among the mid and smaller cap stocks that I owned.

I have also looked at the performance on a quarterly basis. My worst period of underperformance was seven quarters in a row in the late 1980s/early

RELATIVE PERFORMANCE OF FIDELITY SPECIAL SITUATIONS
Year-by year returns: fund versus FTSE All-Share Index

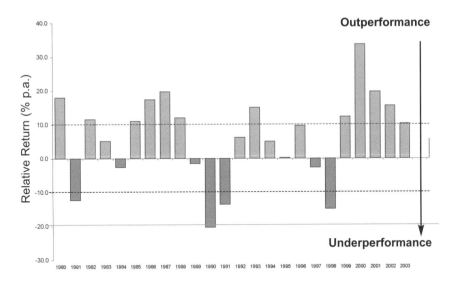

1990s (interestingly, towards the end of this period was the only time in 25 years that Ned Johnson has talked directly to me about the fund's performance!). I have had one period of four quarters underperformance, one period of three quarters and eight periods of two quarters underperformance. Other than these, my poor patches have been limited to one quarter.

What perhaps surprises people most (and maybe surprises me a bit too!) is that there seems to be little correlation between the size of the fund and its relative performance. The fund has benefited in recent years from the strong outperformance by 'value' stocks since the TMT bubble burst in 2000. The tide has been very much flowing with me since then. Looking forward the environment is likely to be tougher and outperformance may be harder to achieve. Nevertheless the fact that both Special Situations and the European fund beat every other unit trust in their first ten years regardless of their area of specialisation remains my proudest achievement. Special Situations has also beaten every other fund since its inception 25 years ago.

Largest holdings

In the appendices you will find a table of the ten largest holdings in the fund on a year-by-year basis, going back to 1981 (see page 152). I think the first observation anyone in the fund management industry might make in looking at these is that you definitely can see that it has lived up to its name as a Special Situations fund. There are many companies in the list which are not well known. The large household names appear only infrequently. In fact there are one or two names that even I remember almost nothing about. For example, what were Vitatron and Debron Investments?

A second observation is that it is a 'warts and all' list. I notice four examples of companies that later failed: Polly Peck (which appeared in 1987, 1988 & 1989), Parkfield (1990), Torras Hostench (1988 – one of the largest corporate failures in Spain but, in this case, I had sold out well before) and Wickes (1993, 1994, 1995 & 1996.) There may be others that I didn't spot. The key point is that my style will always occasionally produce some companies that fail, although each one taught me a lesson and I try not to repeat my mistakes. Despite this the fund can do well if it has enough winners to compensate.

Another thing that sticks out is how certain stocks reappear after a period. Examples include FNFC (which I think I owned in three different periods before it was eventually bought by Abbey National); several TV stocks (LWT, TV-AM, Thames TV, Scottish, Central); gambling companies (Pleasurama, London Clubs, Crockfords) and the two companies (Securicor and Security Services) that part-owned Cellnet, the mobile phone operator, before BT bought full control. There have always been certain franchises I've liked which I will come back to whenever the valuation is attractive enough or they reappear as recovery stocks.

The lessons I have learnt

Investment is not an exact science, and I know of no successful professional investor who has not had to learn from experience the many pitfalls that lie in wait. Over the course of my 25 years in charge of Special Situations, I have had plenty of time to reflect on the factors that matter in becoming a successful stockpicker. These are some of the lessons that I have taken from experience:

- ## Understand the business franchise and its quality

    Businesses vary greatly in their quality and sustainability. It is essential to understand the business, how it makes money and its competitive position. Like Warren Buffett, my ideal is to find businesses with a valuable franchise which can sustain the business over many years. A simple question I ask is: how likely is the business to be here in ten years time – and how likely is it to be more valuable than today?

- ## Understand the key variables that drive the business

    Identifying the key variables that affect a company's performance, and in particular those that it cannot control, such as currencies, interest rates and tax changes, is essential to understanding a share's dynamics. To my mind an ideal business is one that is largely in control of its own destiny. I remember the opposite of this, a UK chemical company I met a few years ago. At one exchange rate it had a prosperous business: but at a higher value of sterling it was totally uncompetitive and possibly had no business at all.

- ## Favour simple over complex businesses

    If a business is very complex, it will be difficult to work out if it has a sustainable franchise. It may need experts to spot a flaw. The ability to generate cash is a very attractive attribute: in fact, the most favourable of all attributes. All else being equal, companies that need a lot of capital expenditure to keep going are less attractive than those that don't. A private equity specialist once told me the stock market overvalues growth and undervalues cash generation. Private equity investors do the opposite. On this measure I'm on the side of the private equity investors.

- ## Hear directly from the management

    Candidness and lack of hyperbole are the key management attributes to look for. In my experience, second hand information is always inferior to first hand information. Having met hundreds of companies in many different industries over the years, the thing I value most is hearing a candid, balanced view of a business. That means the minuses as well as the pluses (all businesses have both). I like managers who do not overpromise but then consistently deliver a bit more than they indicated. Be most wary of those who promise the sky, they are unlikely to deliver. That said, I am in the Warren Buffett camp in that I would rather have a great business run by average management than a poor business run by stars.

- Avoid 'dodgy' managements at all costs

I used to think the dynamics of a strong-looking business would make up even for 'dodgy' management. Having invested in a few companies that have subsequently 'blown up', managements that are either unethical or that sail close to the wind are now complete no-go areas for me. What I've learnt is that, even with corporate governance checks and outside accountants, there are too many ways that senior people can pull the wool over an investor's eyes. Several years ago an Italian contact told me, helpfully, not to touch Parmalat for this reason. It turned out to be an excellent piece of advice. As Warren Buffett says, the CEO who misleads others in public may eventually mislead himself in private (as you are by now well aware I am, like many others, a great Buffett fan. The Berkshire Hathaway annual reports are a treasure trove of investment advice and financial wisdom).

- Try and think two moves ahead of the crowd

Try to identify what is being ignored today which could re-excite interest in the future. The stock market doesn't look very far ahead and therefore, somewhat like chess, looking a bit further out than others often can pay dividends. I think I'm good at knowing the types of situation that will excite investors, where there can be 'blue sky' in the future. I will try to find companies where this is currently being ignored but in my view will impact investor psychology again in the future.

Warren Buffett: "A treasure trove of investment advice."

- Understand the balance sheet risk

  If the stockpicker has to learn only one lesson, this has to be near the top of the list. If investment is about limiting the downside and avoiding disaster, then taking on balance sheet risk should only be done with one's eyes open. Balance sheet risk has been the most common factor behind my worst investments. In my experience, most analysts are poor at assessing this risk and many do not analyse balance sheets at all. As well as debt in its various forms, one needs to be able to analyse pension fund deficits and value redeemable convertible preference shares where there is little likelihood of conversion. Both these have a number of characteristics in common with conventional debt.

- **Seek ideas from a wide range of sources**

  I like lots of ideas from sources I believe to be well informed about particular companies or industries. The more there are to pick from, the more chances you have of finding a winner. The most obvious sources are not always the best. I particularly like sources not widely used by most institutions. On the other hand I'm not proud and pinching an idea from a competitor whom I rate is just as acceptable to me as from a stockbroker!

- **Watch closely the dealing by company insiders**

  No indicator is infallible, but dealings by directors of companies are a valuable confirming or non-confirming tool, particularly look for multiple transactions. Buys are generally more important than sells and some directors have better records than others.

- **Re-examine your investment thesis at regular intervals**

  Investment management is all about building conviction for an investment opportunity and then re-examining this conviction over time, particularly when new information arises. Conviction or strength of feeling is important and should be backed. However, conviction must not develop into pig-headedness. If the evidence changes, so should one's views.

- **Forget the price you paid for shares**

  The price you paid is totally irrelevant; it is only psychologically important. Have no hesitation in cutting losses if the situation changes. A classic example of this was Deutsche Babcock, a German engineering conglomerate that was involved in a number of areas, including shipbuilding. Our analyst who covered the stock came into my office one morning in a very excited state. The chief executive, whom we admired and who had a good record, was leaving the company. He was also planning a management buyout of its best division, shipbuilding, which was the prime reason we owned the shares. I immediately told our trading desk to sell the whole position, aggressively if need be. Although I took a big loss on the position, a few months later the receivers were called in.

- ## Past performance attribution is generally a waste of time

If life is about making mistakes and learning from them, so too is the stock market. However performance attribution, the business of analysing in detail which stock or industry 'bets' a manager has made relative to an index or benchmark, has become very fashionable. However, as it mainly involves looking in the rear view mirror, it tells you nothing about the future. I recognise that with balanced mandates, some attribution is necessary and customers such as pension fund trustees require it.

Often, the tendency is to believe the immediate past is going to be repeated in the future. When one is not doing well, to be constantly reminded of the fact by consultants is rarely a help, and in fact may well be counter-productive! Temperament is important. If you are a manic depressive, don't think of becoming an investor. It is important to treat success and failure with equanimity. On the other hand, analysing your mistakes ("why was I wrong and were there ways of predicting this?") is different and very worthwhile.

- ## Pay attention to absolute valuations

Investors need some sort of reality check to avoid their being sucked into a stock at times of great exuberance. Looking at absolute valuations at times like this will help. I like to buy stocks which within the next two years you can see will be on a single figure price-earnings multiple, or have a free cash flow yield that is well above prevailing interest rates. If you only look at relative valuations, how stocks compare to each other, you can go seriously astray.

- ## Use technical analysis as an extra indicator

I could write a whole chapter on the use of technical analysis (and one day maybe I will). I know it excites widely different views amongst investment professionals. Some are passionate exponents, while others see it as nothing more than hocus pocus. I view it as a framework for help in decision-making. It is one of the factors which helps me decide the size of bet I take. I use it as a confirming or denying factor. So if the technical analysis supports the fundamental analysis, I will be prepared to take a bigger position. If it doesn't I will take a smaller position. I will also re-examine my fundamental views to check we are not missing something if the technical situation deteriorates. I find it more useful the bigger the market capitalisation of a company.

- Avoid market timing and major macro bets

I want to place my bets where I believe I have a competitive advantage. Many commentators have written over the years of the difficulty of timing the market consistently. I've only had a strong market view perhaps five or six times in the last 25 years. Even then, I certainly wouldn't bet my fund on that view. A time I might add a macro input is when I am trying to decide between two shares in an industry, where I think both are fundamentally attractive, but I only want to buy one. A macro view may then be the deciding factor in which to buy (say one benefited from a strong dollar and one did not).

- Be a contrarian!

If the investment feels very 'comfortable' you are probably late. Try to invest against the crowd. Avoid getting more bullish as the share price rises. When nearly everyone is cautious about the outlook, they are probably wrong and things are going to get better. Equally, when very few are worried that is the time to be most wary. I've found the times I can be the most help to some of my less experienced colleagues is when there is great optimism or pessimism. This is when I remind them that the stock market is an excellent discounting mechanism. By the time everyone is worried about something it is normally largely in the price. Investors need to be constantly reminded that this is how markets work.

The future

The question I am most frequently asked is how long I intend to continue to run my UK funds. Stepping down from running my European funds signalled to people that I wasn't going on forever. In fact I have made no secret that I don't intend to go on running my funds into my sixties (I am 54 years old now). However, to avoid speculation that I'm about to give up in the short term, I gave a commitment when I gave up my European funds at the start of 2003 that I would go on running Special Situations and Special Values for at least a further two years. I said I would review this decision annually and at the end of 2004 I extended my commitment by a further year to continue at least until the end of 2006. By the end of 2005 I will decide whether to extend this again for a further year, and so on.

The next thing to say is that, even when I do give up running the funds, I expect to continue to work at Fidelity perhaps on a part-time basis and continue to have an input into the investment process. The one thing I have no intention of doing is leaving to work for a competitor or starting my own hedge fund. As well as an overseeing role on the investment side I hope to be involved in mentoring the younger fund managers and analysts. I have been doing this more since giving up the European funds. I also expect to spend some time on recruiting and marketing.

Finally I would expect to have some input into how we keep ahead of our competitors. As mentioned earlier, my strong belief is that unless you keep on reviewing your competitive advantage and finding new ways to keep ahead, your business will suffer. I am a firm believer in Fidelity's approach of growing future fund managers internally (even though this was not true in my case). Recruiting managers externally can be a risky business, not least because it is extremely difficult in our profession to differentiate between skill and luck in the shorter term.

When we have worked with an analyst for a minimum of five or six years and they have covered at least two different industries, we have an excellent insight into whether they are likely to be a successful portfolio manager in the future. Our 'bottom-up' stock picking approach requires fund managers to have similar analytical skills to our analysts. Proving yourself as an analyst is therefore an essential prerequisite for becoming a portfolio manager. Most of our analysts aspire to be fund managers, but only the best succeed.

The way we will pick a successor for Special Situations is that, during the year before I finally give up, a small group of the senior investment team at Fidelity will choose who we think is the best candidate from our other existing experienced UK fund managers. A cascade effect is likely at that point, as my successor takes over my funds and a new manager in turn takes over their previous responsibilities. This process seemed to work well when I stopped running the European funds. We were able to give about six months notice of who was to take over. We chose two long standing Fidelity managers, Tim McCarron and Graham Clapp, and I am delighted that the good performance of the funds has continued since I have given up running them.

Some observers have asked why we cannot name a successor now and the two of us work together over the next few years. The simple answer is that this is not our approach. What we want to do is pick the best person when the time comes. In the fast changing world of investment, it is possible that someone we choose today will not be the same person we might choose at the appropriate time. The more evidence one has (in terms of time and record), the better.

There are no guarantees in this world but I know our system works and that when I do step down, whenever that will be, we will pick an excellent successor and the fund will be in good hands. In the meantime it continues to be business as usual. Stockpicking has been my professional life, and I can safely say that there is no better or more interesting way to earn a living.

Stockpicking at its best

The performance of Fidelity Special Situations
1979-2004

Introduction

This chapter takes a detailed look at the track record of the Fidelity Special Situations fund, which was formally launched on December 17th 1979. Although Anthony Bolton has managed other funds since, this is the only one for which there is a continuous track record which dates back over the full 25 years of his career at Fidelity. As such it is the best measure of his achievements as a fund manager. His track record in running European equity funds from 1985 to 2003 has also been consistently impressive, though sustained over a shorter period (17 years, 1985-2002).

The chapter falls into six parts, as follows:

- A history and description of the Special Situations fund

- Analysis of its performance over the 25 years 1979-2004

- The fund's risk and style characteristics

- Best and worst moments to buy/own the fund

- The performance of Bolton's European fund 1985-2002

- A summary and conclusions section

The chapter also makes reference to two independent analyses of the fund that were carried out as part of the research for this book. One is an analysis of the fund's track record by Alastair MacDougall, Head of Research at the WM Company, the Edinburgh-based performance and risk analysis consultancy firm. The second, by Lee Gardhouse, the fund of funds manager at Hargreaves Lansdown, the UK's largest fund broking firm, considers the fund's track record from a style perspective.

These two reports are included in full in the Appendix, along with the most recent (October 2004) appraisal of the fund by the ratings agency Standard & Poor's. Unless otherwise stated, all performance data in this chapter comes from Fidelity, and has been verified by them. A spreadsheet containing the monthly source data for the fund, the FTSE All-Share Index and the average performance of funds in the UK All Companies sector can be obtained on request from the publishers.

At one point, shortly before he started handing over responsibility for the European funds to his colleagues Tim McCarron and Graham Clapp, Bolton was managing £10 billion of client money in his UK and European funds, including three of the four largest funds in the Fidelity stable. Had his funds been a quoted investment trust, like for example, the Foreign and Colonial Investment Trust, in 2002, his last year managing European funds, it would have ranked as the 23rd largest company in the FTSE 100 Index, one place below Abbey National.

Even though Bolton has now cut back on his responsibilities, the Special Situations fund on its own in mid-2004 still had a market value equal to the 64th largest company in the FTSE 100 Index, one rank above British Land. According to a survey in Bloomberg Money, the only UK equity fund manager who currently has with more retail investors money to look after is Neil Woodford, who manages a range of equity income funds for Invesco Perpetual with combined assets of nearly £5 billion.

About the fund

The fund was launched in December 1979 and completed its first full calendar month's trading in January 1980. It therefore celebrates its 25th anniversary in December 2004. Depending on the context, the performance data used in this section runs either to December 2003 (24 complete years) or to August 2004 (being the latest month for which monthly data was available at the time of writing).

The fund has grown rapidly in size over the years. In 1984 the fund's net asset value was still less than £10 million. In 1987 it passed £100 million for the first time. In 1995 the net asset value topped £500 million for the first time and then doubled to pass £1,000 million for the first time in 1998. Since then it has more than trebled again in size to reach £3,800 million at the end of August 2004.

The fund now ranks as the largest single unit trust in its sector of the Investment Managers Association rankings. This is the UK All Companies sector: to qualify for inclusion in this sector, a fund has to invest 80% or more of its assets in UK equities and have capital growth as its primary objective. As at August 31st 2004, there were 304 funds in this category.

Special Situations is also the largest fund in the entire 2800-strong unit trust universe.

The growth in the size of the fund has come from two sources: (1) the amount of capital committed by investors; and (2) the performance of the investments controlled by Bolton as fund manager. The net asset figure is struck after deducting the costs of running the fund and marketing it to investors. The size of the fund has grown at a compound rate of 24% per annum over the last seven years.

Fidelity Special Situations is an accumulation fund. That is to say, it does not pay any dividends, but retains and reinvests all investment returns within the fund. The returns to investors are therefore all generated in the form of capital gains. The way that an investor realises his investment is by selling units.[1]

Investors in the fund pay an annual management fee of 1.5% per annum. (The initial management fee of the Special Situations fund was 0.75%, rising to 1% per annum in 1982 and 1.5%, its current level, in 1988). Out of this fee Fidelity has to meet most of the costs of running the fund, including a contribution to the salary of Anthony Bolton and his analyst colleagues, other overhead costs and commission payments to intermediaries who have introduced their client to the fund.

The fund carries an initial fee (buying cost) of 5.0%. In practice a portion of this is often rebated to investors by IFAs and other intermediaries. Fidelity will receive an estimated £60 million in 2004 as management fees for the funds that Bolton manages. At a conservative estimate, Special Situations has grossed more than £200 million in management fees since its launch, making it one of the most successful funds ever launched in the UK.

The number of unitholders in the fund has grown from a few thousand at its launch to more than 250,000 today. The number of clients has roughly doubled since 2001. The average size of each investor's holding is today around £14,000. This is roughly twice the size of the average holding in 1997.

The number of shares owned by the fund has grown to keep pace with its growing size. The current list of holdings runs to nearly 200 stocks, compared

---

[1] To be accurate, for its first five and half years, the Special Situations Trust, as it was initially called, did pay a tiny dividend equivalent to less than 1% of the fund's asset value, but this practice was dropped in August 1985.

to thirty in 1979 and sixty in 1982. The average size of holding in the fund grew twentyfold from approximately £75,000 in 1982 to approximately £15 million in 2000. That is one indication of the change in size of individual investment that Bolton now has to make because of the fund's increased size.

Performance analysis

Any analysis of a fund manager's performance has to be set in the context of the overall dynamics of the stock market and the fund management business. The performance of funds is a controversial subject and one that invites contrasting views. On the one hand are those who say that there is little or no added value in fund management. On the other are those who argue that it is one of the most demanding and difficult jobs in the world and that investors are justified in paying for the services of the best practitioners.

Over the past thirty years, with the publication for the first time of detailed performance records for all publicly owned funds, investors have become increasingly acquainted with a number of uncomfortable facts about the medium and long-term performance of actively managed funds. These facts are ones that many first time investors find disappointing, but which are too well-documented in academic and professional studies to be capable of dispute.

These uncomfortable facts include the following:

1. Most actively managed funds fail to do better than the stock market as a whole over anything but short periods. Over periods of more than five years, a clear majority of funds, typically 70% or more, will fail to beat a comparable broad market index, such as the FTSE All-Share Index. (This is the benchmark that is most commonly used to measure the performance of UK equity funds, including Fidelity Special Situations.)

2. An important reason behind this disappointing performance is the impact of costs (the management fees charged by the fund provider and the transaction costs incurred in trying to beat the market). In many cases these tend to outweigh any advantage that a fund manager may be able to gain by superior stock selection.

3. In fact, academic studies also suggest that it is difficult for professional fund managers to beat the market consistently even before taking account of costs. This is because the stock market is a highly developed and competitive market in which no one individual, however talented and well-informed, can reliably expect to make persistently superior decisions to the majority of other participants in the market.

4. For the same reason even those who do succeed in putting together such a track record, the margin of outperformance is often surprisingly modest. A fund manager who can consistently beat the market by more than 1% per annum after costs is already an exceptional fund manager. Even such stock market legends as Warren Buffett and Peter Lynch only beat the market over the long run by a few percentage points per annum.

Given the availability of low cost index funds as a credible alternative, it follows that finding an actively managed fund that can produce returns after costs that are consistently superior to the market over a period of several years is a challenge. (The time aspect is important because the cost structure of unit trusts normally makes it unwise to buy them unless you are prepared to hold them for at least 3-5 years.)

It also follows that those who have demonstrated that ability consistently are liable to be highly valued by investors. While it is impossible to prove that a fund manager who has been successful in beating the index in the past will do so reliably again in the future, many investors, rightly or wrongly, act on the belief that it is true. It is partly for this reason that regulators insist that all stock market funds are sold with the warning that past performance is not necessarily a guide to the future.

Fidelity Special Situations

In this context, as in other respects, the track record of Anthony Bolton's Special Situations fund stands out as exceptional. The compound annual rate of return from his fund, 19.9% per annum over 24 years to the end of 2003, has beaten the FTSE All-Share Index, its benchmark, by 6.4% per annum over the same period. This is a better record than that of any comparable retail unit trust over the same period.

FIDELITY SPECIAL SITUATIONS: THE 25-YEAR STORY

YEAR	BOLTON	MARKET	PEER GROUP	INFLATION
1980	58.0%	32.9%	28.2%	15.1%
1981	-1.6%	11.8%	13.3%	12.0%
1982	42.9%	27.0%	25.2%	5.4%
1983	34.6%	27.3%	30.2%	5.3%
1984	27.2%	30.2%	27.2%	4.6%
1985	32.8%	18.6%	22.4%	5.7%
1986	47.8%	25.8%	28.7%	3.7%
1987	28.0%	7.3%	13.5%	3.7%
1988	23.1%	10.2%	7.9%	6.8%
1989	32.5%	34.6%	25.3%	7.8%
1990	-28.8%	-10.9%	-13.8%	9.3%
1991	3.1%	19.3%	14.4%	4.5%
1992	26.4%	19.1%	18.3%	2.6%
1993	46.4%	27.3%	28.9%	1.9%
1994	-2.2%	-6.6%	-6.5%	2.9%
1995	23.4%	22.8%	20.9%	3.2%
1996	26.8%	15.7%	16.0%	2.5%
1997	20.1%	23.1%	20.6%	3.6%
1998	-3.2%	13.8%	10.3%	2.7%
1999	39.4%	24.2%	27.1%	1.8%
2000	25.8%	-5.9%	-4.3%	2.9%
2001	3.8%	-13.3%	-13.9%	0.7%
2002	-10.7%	-22.7%	-23.3%	2.9%
2003	33.3%	20.9%	22.1%	2.8%
2004 *	9.2%	2.9%	2.6%	2.1%
AVERAGE	21.5%	14.2%	13.7%	4.7%
MEDIAN	26.4%	19.1%	18.3%	3.6%
HIGHEST	58.0%	34.6%	30.2%	15.1%
LOWEST	-28.8%	-22.7%	-23.3%	0.7%

* Figures to end August 2004.

Notes to Table

The 'Bolton' column summarises the performance of Fidelity Special Situations. The 'Market' column shows the returns for the FTSE All-Share Index (assuming re-investment of dividends). The 'Peer group' column is the average performance of funds in the All Companies sector. The 'Inflation' column measures changes in the Retail Price Index (data courtesy of WM Company).

The annual performance figures for the fund and its benchmark, the FTSE All-Share Index are summarised in the table opposite. Comparative figures for the average fund in the fund's peer group, the UK All Companies sector are also included, along with inflation data for the same period. The analysis in this chapter also makes reference to the monthly performance of the fund and the same comparators over the entire period 1979-2004.

The performance of the fund's investments has been the biggest driver of its growth. The simplest illustration of its success is to say that anyone who invested at the launch of the fund and maintained his or her investment would have around £85 for every £1 invested in 1979. To be more precise, an initial investment of £1,000 in December 1979 would have been worth £76,914.20 at the end of 2003 and £84,001.55 at the end of August 2004.[2]

A £5,000 investment at launch would therefore be worth £420,007.73 (data as at August 31st 2004); and anyone who invested £10,000 would have £840,015.46. Anyone who invested more than £11,905 would now be a paper millionaire on the strength of that investment alone. (If he or she were to realise that investment, there would be capital gains tax to be paid for those who put their money into the fund before the introduction of tax-exempt PEPs and ISAs).

In comparison, an investment in the FTSE All-Share Index, with all dividends reinvested, would have seen every £1 become £20.77 at the end of 2003 and £21.38 at August 31st 2004. An initial investment of £1,000 would today be worth £21,377.50 and an initial £5,000 worth £106,887. The initial investment needed for the stock market as a whole to generate £1 million over the period December 1979-August 2004 was £46,779.

For anyone who invested at the outset, therefore, Bolton's fund has generated some 4.1 times as much money as the UK stock market as a whole has done over the past 25 years. The 4.1 times multiple is the result of two separate effects: (1) his superior performance as a fund manager, and (2) the secondary (but equally important) effect of compounding his superior returns over a period of many years.[3]

[2] This figure allows for an initial buying charge of 3.5%, but excludes the spread, or difference between the bid and offer price, that would be payable if a holding in the fund were to be sold.

[3] Once described by Einstein as the eighth wonder of the world, compounding measures the phenomenon by which year after year of continuous growth can lead to rapid escalation in the end value of a series.

The degree by which the fund has outperformed the market – more than 6% compound per annum over the life of the fund – stands favourable comparison with the track records of famous investors such as George Soros, Warren Buffett and Peter Lynch in the United States. Not surprisingly perhaps, as a result the track record of the fund over 25 years is the best of its kind in the UK.

There are 300 surviving UK unit trusts with history that goes back more than 20 years; of these only 53 invest solely or mainly in the UK stock market. The 20-year return recorded by Fidelity Special Situations is more than twice as good as that of the next best surviving UK equity unit trust. (2,615% at the end of 2003, compared to 1,241% for the second placed fund and 696% for the average surviving UK equity unit trust.)

Performance over time

Only a small percentage of those who bought the fund at its launch have held the fund continuously to the present day. Most of those who own the fund have bought units more recently. More than half the 250,000 investors who own units in the fund have in fact made their investment in the last five years.

What matters to the investors in a fund is not the performance over its whole life, but the pattern of investment returns over the period that they have owned the fund. (History reveals many examples of funds that made spectacular returns when they were first launched, but which subsequently failed to match those returns as they became bigger, and adding value through active management of the portfolio became more difficult.)

The analysis in this section looks at both the absolute and relative returns that the fund has delivered over different time periods, and the rolling performance that it has achieved over every one, three, five and ten year period within its 25-year history. The first series records the results that Anthony Bolton has achieved as manager of the fund. The second describes the returns investors have experienced over different holding periods.

(1) Period by period returns

As can be seen from the table on page 90, in absolute terms the two worst periods of performance of the fund were during the recession of 1990-1991 and in the middle period of the bear market of 2000-2003. In its entire 25-year history, however, the fund has so far experienced only two seriously poor calendar years (1990 and 2002) in which the fund's value has fallen by more than 10%. The average calendar year performance has been 21.5%, outstripping both the FTSE All-Share Index and his peer group.

Given its strong performance, it is not a surprise to find that Fidelity Special Situations has also produced powerful real returns, that is after allowing for the effect of inflation. Real returns are the proper measure of an investment's true value to an investor. Inflation has fallen sharply since the date that the fund was launched. Since 1979 both the fund and the market have produced returns that substantially exceeded inflation.

A different way to track the pattern of a fund's returns over time is to plot the moving average of its returns. This approach smoothes out the year-to-year fluctuations to show its cumulative average performance at any particular date. The more periods that are included, the more representative the trend line becomes. The chart below summarises the trend in yearly performance of the fund, the FTSE All-Share Index and inflation on this measure.

THE FUND, THE MARKET AND INFLATION
Moving average of returns 1979-2004

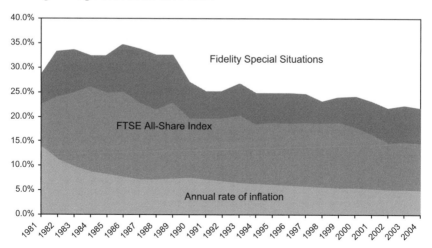

THE PAYBACK TO INVESTORS (1)
Compound rates of return over time

COMPOUND RETURNS BY DATE OF INVESTMENT
Return to end 2003

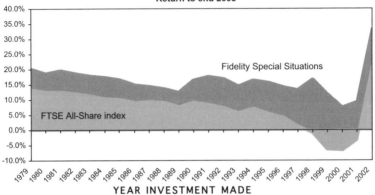

YEAR INVESTMENT MADE

COMPOUND RETURNS BY DATE OF REALISATION FROM LAUNCH
(JANUARY 1ST 1980)

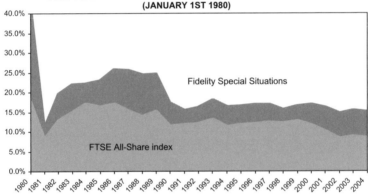

YEAR INVESTMENT REALISED

SUPERIORITY IN COMPOUND RATES OF RETURN
Fidelity Special Situations minus FTSE All-Share Index

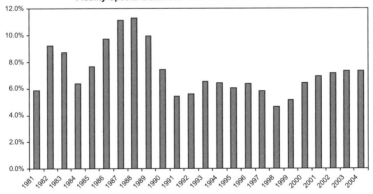

YEAR INVESTMENT REALISED

The track record of the fund can also be measured as the compound annual rate of return achieved over various time periods. The normal way to illustrate this is to calculate the rate of compound growth needed to transform an initial starting sum into today's fund value. The charts on page 94 show the calculations for Fidelity Special Situations and the FTSE All-Share Index for every year since the fund was launched (taking January 1st of each year as the point of investment).

The rate of growth achieved by the fund depends on the start date chosen. It ranges from 33.3% (taking a start date of December 31st 2002) and 7.3% (taking December 31st 2000 as the date of the first investment). In fact, no matter which of the past 25 years an investor first put money into the fund, it would still today be showing a positive return. Regardless of the start date chosen, the investor would also have beaten the FTSE All-Share Index over every period chosen.[4]

The second chart shows compound rate of return data from a different perspective. Instead of showing the rate of return achieved since different investment dates, it shows the rate of return from launch to all subsequent years. In other words, it represents the return achieved by investors who bought the fund at the outset and then realised their investment at some point between launch and the present day.

The data gain underlines the consistency of Anthony Bolton's performance as a fund manager. In fact, closer analysis of the two series reveal that his margin of superiority over the FTSE All-Share Index has actually increased in the last four years. The difference between the compound rate of return recorded by the fund and that of the market index, shown in the third chart, has varied from 4.5% (the lowest margin) to more than 12% (the highest), depending on the choice of start date.

The highest relative compound rate of return has been achieved by investors who put money into the fund at December 31st 1999. They would have received an 11.7% compound rate of return four years later, in a period when the equivalent figure for the FTSE All-Share Index was minus 6.6% per annum. The lowest relative compound rate of return was seen by investors

[4] It may be worth emphasising that these calculations assume that the investment was made on January 1st each year.

who invested at December 31st 1988. Their return to the end of 2003 was 13.8%, while the FTSE All-Share Index produced 9.3%.

(2) Rolling period returns

A more revealing picture of the underlying performance of the fund emerges if you look at rolling 12-month returns (that is, the performance of the fund and the market in each of the 285 successive 12-month periods in its near 25-year history). The top chart on page 97 demonstrates that the performance of the fund has been volatile and follows a cyclical path.

This is something that is a feature of all conventional equity funds, reflecting the volatility of the stock market itself. There have been three periods when the fund has returned more than 80% in a 12-month period and several periods when the rolling 12-month return of the fund has fallen significantly below zero.

Comparing the performance of Fidelity Special Situations with that of the market as a whole, as represented by the FTSE All-Share Index, and employing the same scale, it can readily be seen that the fund has been more volatile than that of the market as a whole. Its best one-year periods have tended to produce much greater returns than the market's best one-year periods, while its periods of poor performance have on occasions, though by no means always, also been deeper than that of the market.

In general, the performance of the fund has been very similar in direction to that of the market and its peer group; in other words, when the stock market as a whole has risen, so too has the fund. When the market is falling, so too in most cases does the value of the fund. This is as you would expect and in line with the findings of standard financial theory that the movement of the market itself is the biggest single influence on any equity fund's performance.

The charts on page 99 show how the fund has performed over longer rolling periods within its 25-year history. The lines track the performance of both the fund and the market over every three-year, five-year and ten-year period within its 25-year history to date. The consistency is again noticeable. For example, the fund has achieved a positive return in nearly 99% of the rolling five-year periods since launch, compared to just under 90% for the market as a whole.

HOW THE FUND COMPARES
Rolling 12-month returns Jan 1980-Aug 2004

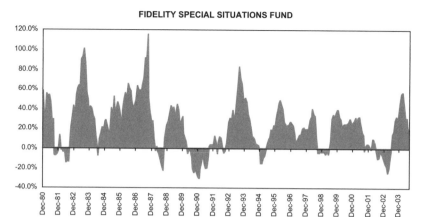

FIDELITY SPECIAL SITUATIONS FUND

END POINT OF 12-MONTH PERIOD

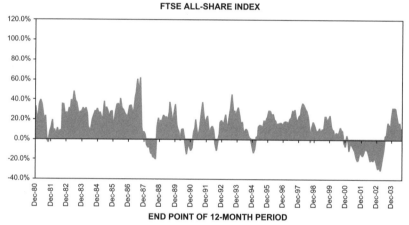

FTSE ALL-SHARE INDEX

END POINT OF 12-MONTH PERIOD

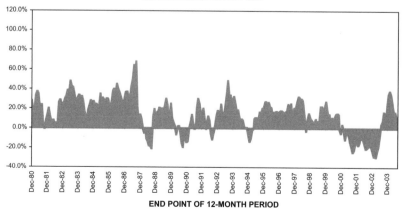

AVERAGE COMPETITOR FUND

END POINT OF 12-MONTH PERIOD

BREAKDOWN OF ROLLING PERIOD RETURNS

	FUND	MARKET	FUND	MARKET	FUND	MARKET
		Month		Quarter		1-year
Average return	1.7%	1.2%	5.2%	3.6%	21.9%	14.1%
Best return	18.0%	13.9%	44.1%	20.9%	115.5%	61.2%
Worst return	-26.8%	-26.5%	-34.4%	-30.1%	-30.0%	-29.8%
		3-year		5-year		10-year
Average return	79.7%	50.3%	168.8%	102.6%	453.4%	279.1%
Best return	366.1%	176.3%	844.9%	320.8%	1459.1%	692.3%
Worst return	-28.9%	-39.3%	-17.6%	-28.8%	155.2%	65.0%

It is also instructive to look at the scale of the absolute returns achieved. Over ten years, whichever month an investor originally put money into the fund, it has never failed to return at least 100% to investors; in fact the lowest ten-year return to date has been 155%. The fund has delivered a 10-year return of more than 200% 96% of the time. The comparable figure for the All-Share Index is 75%. Over five years, the average rolling period return has exceeded 100% 65% of the time.

MARGIN OF PERFORMANCE

% OF PERIODS IN WHICH RETURN WAS:	HOLDING PERIOD IN YEARS							
	3-years		5-years		7years		10-years	
	FUND	MARKET	FUND	MARKET	FUND	MARKET	FUND	MARKET
>50%	69.8%	49.6%	88.2%	81.5%	100.0%	87.9%	100.0%	99.4%
>100%	32.8%	10.3%	65.5%	47.9%	92.6%	80.9%	100.0%	88.2%
>150%	9.2%	1.5%	45.0%	19.7%	71.6%	47.9%	100.0%	84.3%
>200%	2.7%	0.4%	30.3%	8.4%	54.4%	24.7%	96.1%	74.7%

PAYBACK TO INVESTORS (2)
Absolute returns from Special Situations and FTSE All-Share Index

ROLLING 3-YEAR RETURNS

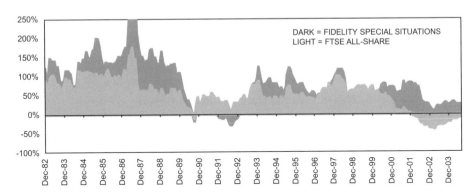

ROLLING 5-YEAR RETURNS

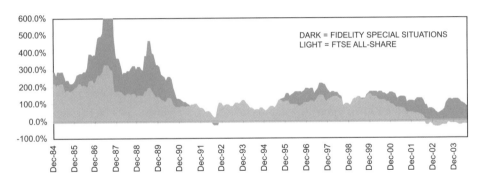

ROLLING 10-YEAR RETURNS

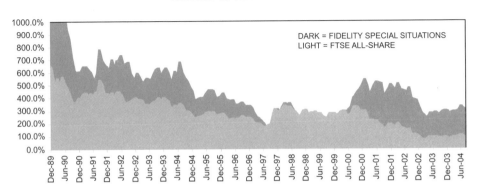

(3) Frequency and peer group analysis

The charts opposite show the average returns from Fidelity Special Situations over different periods, with comparative figures for the FTSE All-Share Index and the average UK equity fund in Anthony Bolton's peer group alongside for comparative purposes. Analysing the frequency of returns gives a more detailed picture of the way its returns are produced.

The data shows that Special Situations has beaten the market by more than 2% in a month 30% of the time and by more than 5% in a single month 10% of the time. Just as importantly, its bad months also tend to be less severe than those of the market. The longer an investor has owned the fund, the more consistently Bolton has beaten the market.

The scale of the return has also been considerably greater. Over five years, for example, investors have recorded a return of more than 50% 88.2% of the time: more than 100% 65.5% of the time, and more than 150% 45.0% of the time. The comparable figures for the FTSE All-Share Index are 81.5%, 47.9% and 19.7% respectively, and for the peer group 76.4%, 43.6% and 24.1%.

The relative performance of the fund can be assessed by looking at its ranking in its peer group. Fund performance is typically measured in deciles (bands of 10%) or quartiles (bands of 25%). A feature of Fidelity Special Situations performance is that while for short periods it resides at the bottom of the rankings, often in the 10% worst performing funds in its peer group, the UK All Companies Sector, over time it invariably moves back towards the top. It features regularly in the top 10% of funds over periods of more than three years.

The charts for relative performance on page 101 underline however that the fund's relative performance against the FTSE All-Share Index has varied considerably from period to period. The biggest margin of outperformance was achieved in the first ten years of the fund's history. Since then there have been periods when both the five and ten-year rolling returns of the fund have fallen behind that of the market as a whole, but these have been the exception rather than the rule.

BEATING THE BENCHMARK
Difference in returns over one, three and five years
Fidelity Special Situations vs FTSE All-Share Index

ROLLING 12-MONTH RETURNS

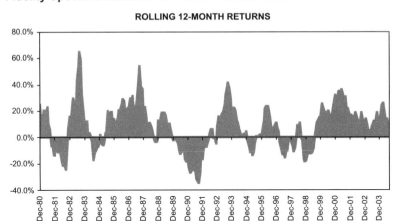

ROLLING 3-YEAR RETURNS

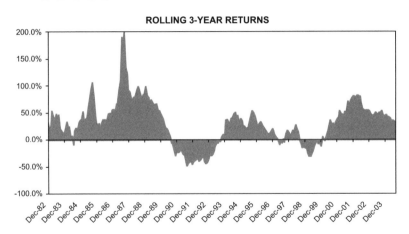

ROLLING 5-YEAR RETURNS

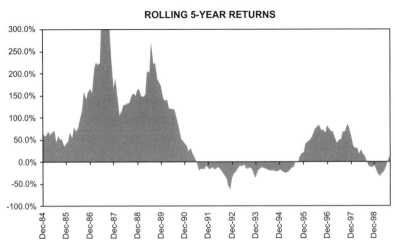

The outperformance in the first ten years of the fund's life is a not uncommon feature of funds that subsequently become large and well-known. In its first few years, the fund had less than £10 million in assets and the portfolio was concentrated on a small number of smaller capitalisation issues. It is much easier for a risk-seeking manager to outperform a broader market index such as the All-Share Index in these circumstances.

This effect undoubtedly was a contributor to the scale of Bolton's superior performance in his first ten-year period. The fund made a gain of 58% in its first twelve months, a return of 280% in its first five years, and 1,459% in its first ten years. Since then, inevitably, the absolute level of returns has declined. It is not possible to sustain returns at that initial level beyond a certain fund size.

What is striking however is that, while producing lower absolute returns, the fund has continued to sustain the same margin of superior results relative to the market and its peer group. Over the twenty years to the end of 2003, Fidelity Special Situations produced a return in percentage terms that was 3.5 times as great as that of the FTSE All-Share Index and 3.8 times as great as the average unit trust in the UK equity sector. The ratio of outperformance against both the index and the average fund in the sector over the last ten years is virtually identical (3.5 and 3.8 times).

Risk analysis

As Bolton himself notes, his fund is riskier than the market as a whole and inevitably tends to produce lumpier returns. That is the way his funds have been marketed and that is the way that he has duly performed. His fund takes more 'active risks' than almost all the other funds in his peer group. Nevertheless, over the full 25-year period, the volatility of the fund, as measured by the standard deviation of its monthly returns, is only around a fifth greater than that of the FTSE All-Share Index (5.72% per month compared to 4.79%).

The fund has never employed borrowed money to increase returns, though its investment trust sister fund Fidelity Special Values has done so on occasions in its 13-year life. A fund that uses borrowed money to boost its capital will show greater gains when markets are rising in value than one which does

RISK PARAMETERS

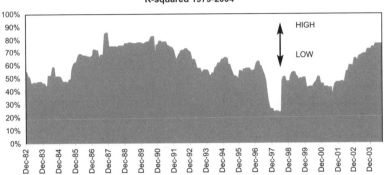

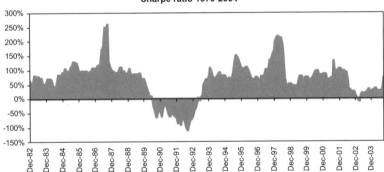

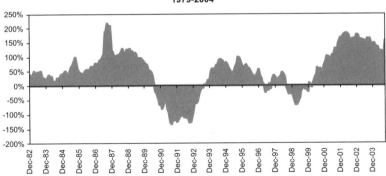

not; and by the same token greater losses when they are falling. Bolton's record with his unit trust is not inflated by gearing.

Because of its superior returns, the fund is one of a tiny minority that have produced positive risk-adjusted returns over the whole 25-year period. It is one of just nine funds, for example, out of the 310 in the UK All Companies sector that produced a positive Sharpe ratio in the three years to the end of 2003. The Sharpe ratio, named after the Nobel prize winning financial academic, William Sharpe, is one of the more commonly used measures of risk-adjusted returns in the fund industry.

The fund has inevitably had several periods when it has done worse than the stock market. The longer an investor holds the fund, as has already been noted, however the less likely it has been to underperform. Over holding periods of seven years or more, whichever month you take as a starting point, the fund has to date always produced a better return than the stock market as a whole.

The fund's worst periods of performance over periods of more than three years have generally also been less severe than that of the market index. This tends to confirm the observation of colleagues that Anthony Bolton's ability to avoid disasters is as great a strength as his ability to pick winners. It is open to argument whether a fund whose worst return over any period of three years or more has been less than that of the market can sensibly be described as a fundamentally riskier fund.

Worst period returns 1980-2004

Holding period	Fidelity Special Situations	FTSE All-Share Index
One year	-30.0%	-29.8%
Two years	-26.6%	-39.9%
Three years	-28.9%	-39.3%
Five years	-17.6%	-28.8%
Seven years	55.4%	9.5%
Ten years	155.3%	65.0%

If however you define risk as its 'tracking error', the extent to which the performance of the fund has deviated from that of the market, as some analysts do, then the fund can indeed be considered higher risk. The graph below is reproduced courtesy of the investment consultants, the WM Company. It shows that Bolton has been highly successful in achieving his stated aim of ensuring that his fund does not mirror the performance of the market, as measured by the FTSE All-Share Index, or that of his peer group.

FIDELITY SPECIAL SITUATIONS AND ITS PEERS

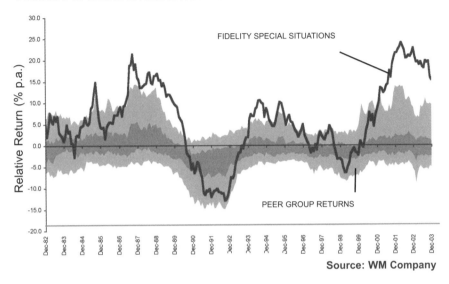

Source: WM Company

A tracking error of more than 10% is unusual in the fund management business. Fidelity Special Situations had a tracking error of 11% over the three years to August 2004. This is substantially higher than almost any other fund in his sector of the fund management business. As WM Company's Head of Research Alastair MacDougall notes, Bolton has been true to the fund's stated intention of not doing the same thing as the rest of the market throughout its life.[5]

A different way to measure how closely a fund mirrors the behaviour of the fund management community as a whole is to look at the degree to which a fund's returns are correlated with those of the market as a whole. Using regression analysis, an advanced statistical technique, it is possible to rank funds on the basis of their correlation with the FTSE All-Share Index. The top chart on page 103 illustrates how this measure, known as r-squared, has moved for Fidelity Special Situations since its launch. The average r-squared for the

[5] See the Appendix, page 132, for a fuller version of MacDougall's analysis.

fund over the 25-year period has been 0.58, with a range between 0.20 and 0.85. A fund that is perfectly correlated with the market will have an r-squared of 1.0. The Special Situations score is very low for its peer group, confirming that Bolton is a genuine contrarian in his investment approach.

Two other standard tools that are used to monitor the behaviour and performance of funds are information ratios and Sharpe ratios. Both analyse how a fund has performed relative to the market on a risk-adjusted basis. In both cases a positive number is the mark of an exceptional fund: the majority of equity funds fail to achieve that. The charts illustrate how Anthony Bolton has consistently produced positive scores on these measures for most of his career, with the notable exception of the 1990-1991 recessionary period and (for the information ratio series alone) in 1998-1999.

The information ratio, if it remains positive over a period of years, is regarded by analysts as the most reliable statistical indicator that a fund's performance is the result of fund manager skill, not merely chance. An information ratio of more than 0.5 is considered worthy of particular attention. Few other UK fund managers have posted such large or positive information ratio numbers (average 0.63, median 0.71) over the past 25 years.

Ranking and information ratio 1980-2003

Year	Quartile	Rank	Year	Information ratio
1980-82	1	5th out of 58	1980-82	0.27
1983-85	1	8th out of 58	1983-85	0.33
1986-88	1	1st out of 94	1986-88	1.42
1989-91	4	87th out of 94	1989-91	-1.15
1992-94	1	3rd out of 154	1992-94	0.82
1995-97	1	12th out of 154	1995-97	0.25
1998-00	1	10th out of 128	1998.00	0.71
2001-03	1	2nd out of 128	2001-03	1.40

Source: WM Company

Style analysis

Many professional consultants also like to analyse the way that a fund performs relative to one or more 'style indices'. The logic here is that in the short to medium term a fund may only be doing well because its particular type of investment style is also doing well. A fund that focuses on buying small capitalisation shares, for example, will usually do better than the market as a whole in periods when small cap shares as a group are also outperforming, and poorly when they are not. In such cases there is no particular skill involved on the fund manager's part.

At other times a fund manager who likes to buy 'value stocks' will do well when 'value' as a style is in favour: and vice versa. Over time these style biases tend to even out, so that a fund that persistently follows one particular style is unlikely to outperform a broad market index over long periods of time. What style analysts attempt to do therefore is to strip out the effects of a fund manager's particular style to find out whether there is anything more to performance than being in the right place at the right time. The way they typically do this is to compare a fund's performance not to a general market index, such as the FTSE All-Share Index, but to indices that reflect the performance of different style groups (small cap and large cap shares, value or growth shares, and so on).

In the case of equity funds such as Fidelity Special Situations, the difference between what a fund actually achieves and the return it could be expected to achieve given its style bias can be interpreted as an indication of the fund manager's skill. An example of the approach is given in the Appendix, based on research carried out by analysts at Hargreaves Lansdown, the UK's largest fund brokerage firm. It is worth emphasising that such exercises are only part of the overall assessment of a fund that analysts carry out.

Nevertheless, the findings for Anthony Bolton confirm that his success cannot be attributed solely, or even at all, to style effects. The following chart compares the performance of the fund to what would have been expected given its bias towards small and midcap stocks. The message is clear: over the period since 1990, when the data series used by Hargreaves Lansdown begins, virtually all of the outperformance achieved by Fidelity Special Situations has come from Bolton's stockpicking ability, not from being exposed to sectors that have outperformed the market.[6]

---

[6] The full analysis can again be seen in the Appendix, this time on page 143.

STOCKPICKING THE KEY TO SUCCESS

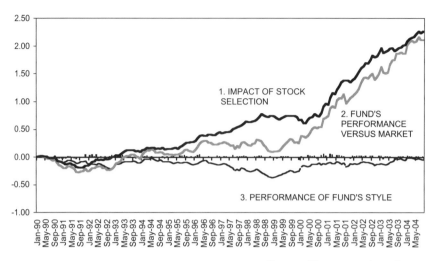

Source: Hargreaves Lansdown

Best and worst years to own and hold the fund

In absolute terms, as already noted, the best year to buy the fund was at its launch. However there have been numerous subsequent opportunities to buy the fund and achieve substantial positive returns. The two worst periods of relative performance occurred around the 1990-91 recession, when the fund experienced poor returns for several quarters in a row, and in the late 1990s when Bolton's value style was out of synch with the market. In the latter case, however, the fund continued to produce strong returns: it was only its performance versus the market that was weak.

For an investor with a truly long term horizon (defined for this example as being ten years) the only period when the fund would have failed to beat the market was if the investor had sold his fund between the end of 1997 and early 2000, having bought it ten years earlier. The worst single month to have bought the fund on this basis was in September 1987, which was the month before the dramatic market crash of October 1987. At that point however the fund, as Bolton has noted, had already risen by 90% in the course of the year, so a correction of some sort was inevitable.

As already noted, the best ten years that the fund has enjoyed since launch were its first ten years, when it was much smaller than it is now and the potential for outperformance was proportionately greater. From launch to December 1989, the fund grew at a compound rate of 31.6%, against the market's 22.2%. In the last ten years (to December 2003) it has grown at a compound rate of 14.5% per annum, against 5.8% for the FTSE All-Share Index.

As a general proposition, the best times to buy the fund historically have been after a period of poor performance. The worst times to buy have been after a period of exceptionally strong performance. This is a pattern that is typical of all the best fund managers and indeed of the stock market in general. (It is a matter of observation however that most investors in practice invest in funds the other way round, buying when a fund has just done well, and shunning the ones which have done relatively poorly.)

Performance of the European fund

A table showing the returns achieved by the Fidelity European fund during Anthony Bolton's time as manager (November 1985 to December 2002) can be found on page 110. The chart below, which shows the rolling 3-year performance of the fund against its benchmark, the MSCI Europe ex UK index, underlines the strong and consistent performance of the fund. The pattern of returns follows that of the UK fund for most of the time, underlining that the two funds have been managed in a broadly similar fashion.

RELATIVE PERFORMANCE IN EUROPE
Fidelity European versus benchmark 3-year rolling returns (%)

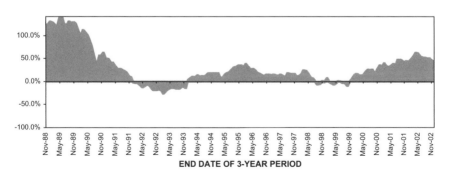

PERFORMANCE OF FIDELITY EUROPEAN
Under Anthony Bolton's management

Year-by-year figures

YEAR	FIDELITY EUROPEAN	MSCI EUROPE EX UK	DIFFERENCE IN RETURN
1985	20.6%	19.3%	1.3%
1986	72.8%	40.7%	32.1%
1987	-7.9%	-29.8%	21.9%
1988	62.8%	31.5%	31.3%
1989	56.4%	38.2%	18.2%
1990	-23.9%	-21.1%	-2.8%
1991	8.2%	19.3%	-11.1%
1992	8.6%	15.2%	-6.6%
1993	61.7%	36.5%	25.2%
1994	-5.7%	-6.5%	0.8%
1995	29.2%	30.1%	-0.9%
1996	22.6%	12.4%	10.2%
1997	22.1%	24.4%	-2.3%
1998	23.5%	27.3%	-3.8%
1999	27.0%	12.2%	14.9%
2000	20.3%	10.5%	9.8%
2001	-10.9%	-24.9%	14.0%
2002	-6.3%	-27.9%	21.5%

Notes:

1985 = two months

2002 = eleven months

Summary and conclusions

The performance of the Special Situations fund under Anthony Bolton's stewardship stands out. This is true both in absolute terms (the gains he has made for his investors) and in relation to other fund managers and the benchmark index against which the majority of UK equity fund managers are measured. More striking still has been the consistency of his performance and the surprisingly favourable risk characteristics. On measures such as information and Sharpe ratios, the fund's record has also been exceptional.

Key points that emerge from analysis are as follows:

- The performance of the fund has declined in absolute terms since its early years. This in part reflects the exceptional returns achieved in its first ten years and the problems of growing fund size, but also the impact of falling inflation, which has been the biggest secular economic trend of the last 25 years. Over time, when inflation and interest rates come down, it is inevitable that nominal returns from the stock market must in due course come down as well.

- Despite this, the margin of outperformance that the fund has achieved relative to the stock market as a whole has been remarkably consistent. The same goes for its performance in real terms (that is, after adjusting for inflation). In fact, because the fund has done so well during the difficult conditions of the bear market, the margin by which Bolton has beaten the market has increased in the last few years.

- The fund has sustained its performance throughout most types of market conditions. Its worst periods for absolute performance were in the recession of 1990-91, when it fell in value by 33.3% from its peak in August 1989 to the trough in January 1991. Over its 25-year history it has experienced seven down years, but in only two of these years was the loss greater than 10%.

- In relative terms, the fund has also had a number of periods when it has underperformed the stock market as a whole. The most extended of these was in the middle to late 1990s. This was a period when the bull market was reaching its apogee and large capitalisation stocks (in which Bolton rarely invests) were much more in demand that the small and midcap stocks which he favours.

- Detailed analysis of the monthly returns of the fund shows that its strike rate (of winning months to losing months) is around the same as the average fund manager in his peer group. The crucial difference is that the fund's average monthly performance in positive months is greater than that of both his peers and the market, while the down months are no worse than either group.

- Over every ten-year holding period, whichever month an investor chose to put their money into the fund, it has never yet failed to produce a return of less than 150% ten years later. While there have been ten-year periods in which the fund has done less well than the stock market as a whole, they have been only two of them, and only one (during the severe recession of 1990-91) that lasted more than three months.

Anything but a lemming

Assessing the Anthony Bolton phenomenon

The performance conundrum

The previous section has analysed the performance of Anthony Bolton's UK Special Situations fund in great detail. For those who appreciate the dynamics of the investment business, the message from the data is an unequivocal one. The track record of his funds over 25 years has been a genuine phenomenon, and one that validates the high regard in which he is held by his professional peers. Three things in particular are striking: the consistency of his fund's performance; the fact that he has managed to build a comparable track record in two major markets (the UK and Europe) at the same time; and the fact that he has been able to sustain his track record despite now running a fund that has grown so big that it dwarfs almost every other in the retail fund sector.

How then can this exceptional performance be explained? And what lessons can investors draw from his success? In this chapter we will examine that question from a number of different perspectives, including canvassing the views of those who have worked most closely with him. Bolton would be the first to admit that he has benefited from running in his fund during a period that has mostly been exceptionally favourable to equity investment. The long and powerful bull market that ran from 1982 to 2000, fuelled by strong disinflationary impulses, was without question the best period in which to own shares in the 20th century. Over those 18 years the annualised return from the stock market (11% per annum in real terms) was 50% greater than the long run historical average for equity investment. It was clearly an exceptional time to be a fund manager; and if ever there was a time to set up shop as a stockpicker, the beginning of the 1980s was that time. The bull market created powerful tailwinds for an aggressive risk-seeking fund manager of Bolton's type.

It was also, we can see now, his good fortune to have the chance to join a world class fund management house just at the point it was launching its push into Europe. At the time, as we have seen, there was no guarantee that Fidelity would enjoy the success that it has done subsequently. In 25 years the firm has gone from nowhere to the number one position in the UK unit trust business, where it has an 8% market share. Although its primary focus remains the private investor market, it has also made inroads into the institutional market. As events have turned out, there can have been few more congenial or supportive environments in which to pursue a stockpicking career. As a privately owned company whose sole business is fund management, Fidelity has been able to avoid the internal battles and multiple changes of ownership that often bedevil the lives of fund managers elsewhere.[1] Its business model has proved to have real and enduring staying power, something that any active fund management house needs if it is to see off the competitive challenge of indexing.

By his own admission, the Fidelity way of doing business, with its focus on research-led equity investment, has suited Bolton well. "Investment people are well protected in Fidelity", says Richard Timberlake, Bolton's first boss, who now runs a fund of funds business that brings him into regular contact with all the main fund management groups. "They don't get drawn into the marketing or administration of the business. Most other fund managers spend a huge amount of their time doing marketing, doing their own admin and doing their own client service. If you can separate the three elements, investment, IT and administration, and marketing, and you can find the best team in each area, and rely on the others to do the other bits, you have a much greater chance of creating a good organisation. In recent years Anthony has been strongly supported by good analysts. I think he is good at getting what he wants from them."

According to Barry Bateman, the Vice Chairman of Fidelity International, the company deliberately puts tight constraints on how much time their fund managers can spend away from their core task, which is picking stocks. The rule inside Fidelity is that no fund manager is allowed to do more than one week a year of marketing, though in practice this is not always as rigorously observed as the rule implies. Bolton, notes Bateman, has always been assiduous about contacting clients and their advisers to explain the background to the performance of the fund, especially when the numbers he has just turned in are less good than normal. "Whereas most fund managers who have a bad patch tend to hide away until their performance improves", he says, "Anthony always makes a special effort to keep in contact with clients and advisers when he has a bad patch."

---

[1]It may be no accident that the American group Capital International, which is widely regarded as one of the most successful of modern fund management groups, is also a private company with a strong internal culture and no distractions from the central fund management effort.

But neither the happy circumstance of his time running money coinciding with a glorious bull market, nor the good fortune of landing his job with such a favourable employer, can fully explain Bolton's success in beating the market so consistently over so many different phases in the market cycle. The fact that he continued to outperform the market by the same margin during the savage bear market that succeeded the bullish conditions of the years up to 2000 is testament to the fact that his working methods capture something that other fund managers seem to lack. Although he has had poor patches in relative terms, some lasting 18 months or more, the longer the holding period in his fund, the better and more consistent its performance has been. The numbers show that, whichever month they bought it, any investor who bought the Special Situations fund in the last 25 years has beaten the market if they held it for seven years or more. This is a more remarkable statistic than it might at first appear.

How others see it

Canvassing the opinions of those who have worked closely with Bolton over the years produces a number of explanations for what it is that has helped to make his time as a fund manager so successful. Every one that I have spoken to have talked eloquently about how hard he works and the discipline with which he approaches his job. According to Sally Walden, who has worked alongside him for more than twenty years, Bolton manages his time extremely carefully. "He is not the kind of guy who lingers for a chat at the coffee machine. He goes out of his way to make sure that no part of his working day is wasted. While he is never unpleasant to anyone, he has the knack of letting you know, in the most charming way, when he has got what he wants from you." Graham Clapp, who took over the running of the offshore European funds from Bolton in 2003, is one of several colleagues who have marvelled at the way that Bolton will immediately dive into a thick wad of research notes the minute his train or plane journey begins.

Drawing on his many years of working with fund managers, Timberlake says that one of the keys to Bolton's success has been his uncanny ability to measure and interpret what the market's expectations for a share are. "The most important thing to understand about Anthony, in my view, is that he is two-brained. Good fund managers are not usually the first class degrees in maths, or someone who is a brilliant accountant or actuary. They usually make poor fund managers. It is far more important to understand crowd psychology, which is a creative skill. A degree in crowd psychology is a far better qualification than being an accountant or an economist. People who are both right and left brained, as Anthony is, are the ones you want. Not only has he got a first class all round brain, but he also understands the market and crowd psychology. He has a creative side that understands other people's behaviour."

Alex Hammond-Chambers, the chairman of the Fidelity Special Values investment trust, agrees. His view is that Bolton has "the most uncanny knack for understanding what the market is discounting in a stock. There aren't many people who can look at a stock and immediately understand what the market's view is. People think they do. You ask 90% of people what the market thought of Vodafone in March 2000 and they would have been wrong. But Anthony has an instinctive understanding of what the share price is telling him the market thinks about a company, and with his perception and experience, he knows whether to agree or not. If he doesn't agree, then that's a buying opportunity."

Simon Fraser, who has worked with Bolton for more than 20 years, and is now Fidelity's Chief Investment Officer, says that his colleague's confidence in buying unloved stocks is underpinned by his acute sense of what the value of a business is, not just to the stock market but to potential trade or private equity investors as well. "One reason that he is happy to buy illiquid stocks that nobody else is prepared to touch", says Fraser, "is that he knows from his innate sense of value that one day someone will come along and bid for them." His success in finding stocks that are later taken over suggests that this is well-founded. In one miraculous year (1999), 30 companies that he owned that year were the subject of takeover bids or some other form of corporate activity. Fraser adds that Bolton not only has the priceless gift of being able to spot an opportunity, but also the courage and decisiveness to act upon that instinct before it is too late. "At the end of the day successful investment is about seeing things more clearly than the rest of the market and acting on them before everyone else has come to the same conclusion. Anthony has the ability to do it, not just think or talk about it."

The most important thing about Bolton, however, says his colleague Sally Walden, is his temperament, which is unshakeably implacable. A good deal of his intelligence, she thinks, is internalised. "He is a very difficult person to read. What he says always sounds very simple, even simplistic. Quite frankly there a lot of fund managers out there who sound a whole lot better when they get up to speak. But none of them has done anything like as well. Anthony is very dispassionate. Whatever happens, he just gets on with the next job on his list. In my view, there is no question that he is a better fund manager today than he was 15 years ago." Barry Bateman, makes the same assessment.

While there is nothing accidental about the success that Bolton has enjoyed, Bateman thinks, what is more easily overlooked is the contribution he has made to the success of Fidelity's international business, not least in establishing a style for the way in which the company operates. "Aside from his performance, which has obviously been exceptional, the fact that Anthony is such a nice guy, quiet and not in any way a prima donna, has helped to set the tone for the whole investment operation. Let us face it, many so-called 'star' fund managers can be unreasonable and difficult to manage. We haven't had that problem, and in large part that is because Anthony has set such a tremendous example. The rest of us have had to follow the same style. Our fund managers are in general easy to manage, fit in well, and are very supportive of the company. A lot of that has been down to the way that Anthony has set the example. It has made an enormous difference to us."

At the same time, says Bateman, he has been struck by how successfully Bolton has made use of the resources that Fidelity places at the disposal of its top fund managers. "For example, we were one of the first groups to professionalise the investment seminar. If you are going to do roadshows, in our view you have got to do them well, to make them the best in the business. The real cost is the time. Year in year out Anthony would do the roadshows, not just in the UK, but in Europe, Taiwan, Australia. It was his commitment to being visible that helped to build the fund and his reputation." Another thing Bolton did in the early days, says Bateman, was spend a lot of time with other parts of the organisation. "We had a big phone sales operation, for example, and he would come down more often than any other fund manager to talk to the phone reps about his fund. He has always spent time with the rest of the group telling them what he is doing. He is the most visible of all the fund managers we have. He has a tremendous commitment to Fidelity and the people here. That has helped the business, but it has also helped Anthony as people are more aware of him and give him more support." That proved particularly valuable in 1990-91 when the fund was threatened with a wave of redemptions after its run of poor performance.

The qualities great investors need

Peter Jeffreys, who worked alongside Bolton in his early days at Fidelity before leaving to co-found Fund Research with Timberlake, says there is no question in his mind that Bolton is one of the few true 'greats' in the UK fund management industry. "There are a number of attributes common to all good fund managers – knowledge, skill, enthusiasm, dedication and 'love of the game', to list only the more obvious ones. Great fund managers, however, have something extra, something less easily definable, which sets them apart from the field". Bolton shares a number of these attributes with Peter Lynch, with whom, says Jeffreys, he can validly be bracketed. "The most important one I would say is that both are their own men. Anyone who has worked with Anthony will know he possesses an independence of mind that is second to none. When researching a company, he will draw on the widest possible range of fact and opinion, but his final analysis will be driven solely by his judgement of a situation, a company's future prospects, or a share's valuation. He will not be influenced by fashion or fad, or the current market view."

Alex Hammond-Chambers, who carried out his own analysis of Bolton's performance shortly after being appointed the chairman of Fidelity Special Values, the sister investment trust to Fidelity Special Situation, says there are many analogies that you can use about good fund managers. "Jimmy Gammell [the founder and guiding light of the Edinburgh investment house Ivory & Sime] always said that the best analogy was sailing; even though you went sailing from point A to point B, you didn't always just go in a straight line. Sometimes you tacked, sometimes you ran, and sometimes you reached. Sometimes, because the winds were very vicious, you had to pull in a reef or two. In other words, you had to adjust your sail and your sailing to the conditions. That's what investment brains do very well, and that's what Anthony does very well. I think he has a very good hand on the tiller."

In fact, says John Chatfeild-Roberts, who runs a successful fund of funds operation for a rival fund management company, Jupiter Asset Management, and has invested in Fidelity Special Situations for many years, Bolton is a rare example of the 'complete' fund manager. The things Chatfeild-Roberts and his team look for when seeking out the best fund managers are "capacity and desire for hard work, the ability to spot opportunities and act on them quickly and decisively, and the imagination to see further ahead than most around you". Bolton has all three in strong measure. "If you see him on the train home, you will find him reading research which, when read, he then deposits in the litter bin before alighting at his station; this is still as true today as it was twenty years ago. Opportunities? Over the years there have been themes that ran through his portfolio. A recent example was the Lloyd's insurance vehicles, which many people didn't believe, or if they did, sold them too soon to reap the full rewards. Imagination? Well you only have to look at the long term holding in Nokia from the early 1990s, when mobile phones were bricks and most people (myself included) swore blind that we would never countenance having such interruptions. What would we all do without them now? Any one of these abilities may make a good fund manager, but to have all three makes a great one".

Chatfeild-Roberts also speculates that there might be something in the fact that Bolton likes to compose music in his spare time. "It has been found that if you play classical music to babies in the womb this stimulates the parts of the brain responsible for both musical ability and mathematical skills. Anecdotal evidence also suggests a strong link between music and maths. In the University of Oxford, maths students approaching their final exams are reported to have a preference for attending Bach recitals. An innate appreciation of pattern in number – which might appear in something mundane as company financial statistics – may therefore be something which helps give Anthony an edge."

Hammond-Chambers adds: "It is the amount of thought that goes into the investments Anthony makes and his ability to think differently from the crowd that more than anything else has enabled him to spot value in a stock in a way that others cannot. The thing I noted was how incredibly few failures he has. He doesn't bomb. He doesn't make big mistakes. I think that's in part because he's so value conscious, so many of the investments he makes don't have a huge big downside. He doesn't chase popular stocks. I'm sure he makes mistakes – we all do – but you need to look at his gains/losses ratio. You normally reckon that a very good portfolio manager is going to get perhaps six pluses, two equals and two minuses for every ten stocks he owns. That will certainly be enough to produce good returns. Anthony does better than that, with the emphasis on very low minuses."

This in turn plays well with those who make their living out of selling funds. Mark Dampier, head of research at Hargreaves Lansdown, a Bristol-based stockbroker that has grown to become the largest player in the fund broking business, says that while Bolton exudes self-confidence, he lacks the arrogance that is so often the downfall of fund managers. "His style of management is difficult to pin down, but his ability to look at stocks in a different way to the market as a whole seems to be his real talent. In other words, he believes in his own valuation techniques, rather than those employed by others." His investment process, finding cheap stocks that the market has overlooked, is not complicated. "While this style can go out of fashion over certain stock market cycles, particularly when we are in recession, he bounces back strongly and makes up for any losses when it does come back into style. Investors have tended to forget that after the stock market crash of 1987, and through the recession of the early 1990s, Anthony's performance was relatively poor. In order to make money with his fund, you have to be patient and hold him through the hard times. He has rewarded you amply if you do this."

The scale of the achievement

Picking one's way through these various ideas, and seeking to assess the true scale of Bolton's achievement, it has to be said that few fund managers stay in the same job, or in charge of the same fund, for 25 years, as he has done. His longevity in the job ensures that his record will stand out to some extent in any comparison of long term performance. It is notable that he has never been tempted to leave Fidelity for a more lucrative alternative, though there have been no shortage of offers. By his own testimony, and those of his colleagues, Bolton likes the freedom that running a successful fund brings. He has been less happy running institutional money, such as pension funds, where the intrusion of consultants and others trying to 'second guess' the decisions made by fund managers is a constant irritation.

Just as importantly, Bolton has demonstrated the stamina and determination to continue in the same demanding job far longer than the majority of his peers. While there have been many fund managers who have racked up strong performances over a period of five or even ten years, a good number of them have found the relentless pressure such a career entails too great and either left the business for less arduous careers, or moved into management.[2] By contrast Bolton has stuck to his last, despite running both UK and European funds for 17 of his 25 years at Fidelity. Although he has now cut back on his European responsibilities, in part to save on all the travelling involved, his staying power is worthy of note. It may be a somewhat trite observation, but in order to produce an exceptional long term track record as a fund manager, you first have to make sure you complete the course, and that Bolton has done.

As the professional analyses quoted in the performance chapter makes clear, no matter which way you analyse the figures, it is difficult to explain away his performance figures by attributing them to risk and style effects. It is true that Bolton has always taken what consultants like to call a lot of 'active risk' in his funds. They have always had a low correlation with the stock market indices. His portfolios look less like the FTSE All-Share Index than almost anybody else's. This was a conscious decision, as Bolton set out from the beginning to take the risk of backing his own judgement about the value of individual stocks against that of the rest of the market. In that narrow sense, the 'active risk' helps to explain how his fund has been able to produce much higher returns than the market and his peers. But simply doing something different from the market is not a sufficient explanation of his success: if being an out-and-out contrarian were such a surefire route to outperformance, you can be certain that everyone else in the industry would be doing the same thing. The reason they don't is that it is very difficult to be both contrarian and right. The usual consequence of taking a lot of active risk in fund management is that it leads to greater underperformance, not greater outperformance.

---

[2] "Promoted to become overhead" in the phrase of Simon Fraser, Fidelity's chief investment officer.

Anthony Bolton: "he possesses an independence of mind that is second to none."

It is certainly possible to explain some periods of his outperformance of the market by looking at the investment 'style' of his fund. Since the bear market ended in 2000, for example, there has been clear evidence that the market has rewarded value investors such as Bolton more than other styles of investor. That is one reason why he has done so well, just as his lack of exposure to large capitalisation stocks in the latter half of the 1990s, and his refusal to pay absurd prices for overhyped Internet stocks, explains why his performance lagged the market quite badly for a while during that time. But what 'style analysis' cannot explain is how Bolton has managed to produce superior performance over the whole 25 year period he has been in charge of Special Situations, and for virtually every rolling five and seven year period within that total as well. The reason is that style differences tend to cancel each other out over time; and as the analysis quoted in the previous section shows, over the longer term the outperformance he has achieved comes almost exclusively from his stockpicking ability, not from the style of the fund.

The importance of being a contrarian

In any event, Bolton's philosophy is to go where he thinks the bargains are, regardless of what impact they may have on his style. His primary objective is to make sure that he never merely buys what everyone else is buying at the time. It is evident that this contrarian approach is one of the keys to his success: yet for those who define 'risk' as the extent to which a fund's holdings deviates from the market, there is little choice but to conclude that Bolton's methods are intolerably risky. The counter-argument to that, one deployed by Warren Buffett among others, as well as Bolton himself, is the common sense cry of the value investor down the ages. The best way for an investor to minimise the risk in a portfolio, they would say, is (1) to diversify, by buying a broad range of stocks: and (2) to buy only shares that are cheap in absolute terms. How can buying things for less than they are worth be riskier than buying everything that everyone else is buying regardless of price? It doesn't make sense.

The data supports this: Bolton's strike rate of successes to failures in stockpicking, consistently near to 70%, is better than virtually all his contemporaries, and the maximum drawdown in his fund – the biggest peak-to-trough decline the fund experiences in down markets – is often lower than the market as whole, not higher as it should be if it was so much riskier. If his funds are more volatile than the market, according to statistical analysis, this may only tell us that the academic measure of volatility is an inadequate proxy for what risk actually means in investment terms. Given the uncompromising nature of the evidence about the inability of the fund management profession in aggregate to outdo the market over long periods of time, it is right to look for alternative explanations when exceptions do appear. But in this case it is as fatuous to try and explain away the success of Bolton's funds by their riskiness as it is to blame it all on good fortune and timing. The evidence does not support the conclusion.

One is left then to ponder some imponderables in seeking the causes of Bolton's success. Hard work and a devotion to his calling are two of his more obvious qualities, but, admirable though they are, they are shared by many of his competitors who have done much less well. While they may be necessary conditions to explain his success, they are clearly not sufficient to do so. The knowledge and discipline that Fidelity's team of analysts provide is clearly another important factor, and essential to the task of running such a big fund as Special Situations has become, Bolton plainly could not have done what he did without the resources of a Fidelity behind him. Again however that can hardly be the whole answer – other fund managers have enjoyed the same resources within Fidelity, but failed to achieve such exceptional results. More important than the scale of the resources available to Bolton perhaps has been the fact that he has been able to mould his support team to provide precisely the information that he requires, at the time and in the form that he needs it.

Most crucial of all, it seems likely, has been the willingness of his employers at Fidelity to allow him a free rein to continue investing in a way that few other companies could in practice tolerate for long. Consistently betting against the rest of the market is by its nature bound to produce occasional bad periods of performance; experience suggests that all large businesses are uncomfortable moving too far out of line with what their peers are doing. It may be no coincidence that many of the true greats in investment, the likes of Buffett, Templeton and Soros, all of whom are essentially contrarians at heart, work in environments where they are able to do what they feel is right, free of corporate constraints and the dead hand of management by committee. That is also why the best fund managers often end up owning their own fund management or advisory business. Bolton's exceptional performance over the years may have something to do with the fact that he not only works for a company that is dedicated to giving fund managers the fullest possible support, but was himself instrumental, as one of its first two fund managers to be appointed in London, in shaping the style and methods of the UK operation over the past 25 years. The temptation to leave and start his own fund has been easier to resist as a result.

In the end however, there is no escaping the fact that active fund management is a little like professional golf – a field where the mediocre can earn handsome rewards, but where true champions, who can raise and keep their game at a higher plane for years at a time, are few and far between. Beating the markets is a tough game, and any individual fund manager who tries to get to the top has to perform in daily competition with some of the brightest, best educated and most highly incentivised people to be found in any profession. It takes rare gifts to sustain success in this business over more than a few years, but the challenge to a certain type of individual is irresistible. Modest and unassuming though he is, it is evident that Bolton has an ideal temperament to pursue his contrarian investment style; dedicated, unflappable, thoughtful, even somewhat obsessed. It takes courage and commitment to go on, year in year out, taking a different view to everyone else in your profession. As the author John Train says in his outstanding study of successful professional investors of the modern era: "Although a professional investor can sometimes strike it rich with a big coup, there's no luck in professional portfolio investing, any more than in master chess. It's a skilled craft, involving many decisions a week. The year-in, year-out manager of a large portfolio can no more pile up a superlative record by luck or accident than one can win a chess tournament by luck or accident."[3]

It is the nature of things for any field of activity to throw up exceptional talents once in a generation, and all the evidence suggests that Bolton is one such individual. It may well be, as he himself concedes, that his performance will flatten off a little in the next few years. It would be no surprise if it were to do so, especially as some of the favourable tailwinds in the market that have helped him recently, such as the return to favour of small and midcap shares as a class, start to reverse. So powerful has Bolton's record as a stockpicker been, however, that even if he were to experience another nightmare year like 1990, and his fund was to fall by 40% in a year, while the market fell by just half that amount, his investors would still be several percentage points – and many thousands of pounds – ahead of the market for those who bought the fund more than five years ago. It would in fact take a quite horrendous reversal of fortune to destroy his reputation now. Even in such an unforgiving business as fund management, where you are only as good as your last set of performance numbers, only the foolhardy would bet against his reaching his chosen retirement date with his reputation as one of the supreme stockpickers of his generation firmly intact.

---

[3] John Train, author of Money Masters of Our Time

General lessons for the investor

It is a generalisation, but a safe one, to say that few investment funds are quite as good as those who promote them claim them to be. A combination of academic studies, a crackdown by regulators on misleading advertisements and the wider availability of industrywide performance statistics have all combined to explode much of the mystique that once surrounded so-called 'star' fund managers. The majority of actively managed funds, as has been noted, fail to beat the stock market averages over any length of time; and those that do often turn out to have done so only because they have taken more risk than the market as a whole. The extra risk tends to catch up with them in the end, exposing the shortcomings of their approach and bringing them crashing back to earth. In the majority of cases, investors who buy actively managed funds would have been better off buying a cheap and efficient index-tracking fund instead and saving on the higher expense that putting their money with an active fund manager entails.

In practice, despite the advent of sophisticated risk and performance analysis systems, there is little evidence that most people who buy funds do so in a particularly educated manner. Figures from the industry show that sales of individual funds are often closely correlated with the league tables of most recent performance. Those funds that produced the best returns in the previous year, or over the previous three years, are typically the ones that most investors want to buy and the ones, less creditably, that most advisers, like to recommend. This is despite repeated warnings from regulators and academics alike that there is no convincing evidence that past performance in funds persists from year to year. Most studies show that the future performance of funds is largely independent of what has gone before: the probability that good historic performance will persist into the future is no different from the probability you would obtain by assuming that performance in the future is a random outcome.[4] In other words, you might as well throw dice to decide which fund to buy.

Fidelity Special Situations clearly is one fund that can demonstrably justify that it has been worth the extra expense of active management. Anyone who

---

[4] One of the few statistically significant exceptions to this observation in some studies of fund performance is that there is a slightly greater chance that a very poor performing fund will continue to do badly than throwing a dice would suggest.

bought the fund on the strength of Anthony Bolton's performance to date would not have been disappointed, provided they held it for a number of years: whichever year between 1980 and 2003 that an investor bought the fund, it would have produced a higher return than the stock market over a subsequent seven-year period. The first and self-evident lesson that emerges from the history of Fidelity Special Situations is therefore that there are some actively managed funds which rightly deserve the support of investors. Even if the chance of finding a fund that can consistently beat the market is odds against, there is nothing illogical about a fund investor seeking to buy a fund that holds out the prospect of producing nearly four times as much money as the stock market as a whole over the following ten years, as Bolton's UK fund has done.

What it is important, secondly, for investors to remember however is that funds such as Fidelity Special Situations are the exception rather than the rule. While its track record is as good as – if not better than – that of every other fund in the UK unit trust business, the real issue that investors have to face is whether they can realistically identify such winners in advance: and if so, how best to set about doing so. (There are other fund managers who have done exceptionally well running hedge funds, or other privately-held funds, but their performance is not directly comparable, and the figures are not always as easy to obtain and analyse). This leads on to a further conclusion: that the secret of finding exceptional funds can only lie in undertaking the most thorough research into the methods and personality of those who run them. It is not enough to rely on past performance figures, nor even on one of the many fund ratings services that now rank funds on a mixture of performance and qualitative measures. One reason why Bolton has earned the support of so many financial advisers is that he has spent 25 years explaining what he does in great detail to anyone who will listen. The logic of his approach, coupled with his patent personal integrity, have been as important as his performance track record in winning loyal supporters.

A third conclusion is that the argument about whether actively or passively managed funds are best is something of a red herring. While the emergence of passively managed index funds has undoubtedly been the big story of the past 30 years in investment, the reality is that both types of fund – active and passive – have their rightful place in an investor's armoury. Neither approach is inherently superior to the other.[5] The fact that both types of fund are now widely available adds usefully to the choices that investors face. It is increasingly common for professional investment institutions to adopt a mixed approach to constructing portfolios for clients, with a 'core' element of low cost indexed funds reinforced by a leavening of carefully chosen actively managed funds. This is an approach that can usefully be adopted also by private investors, should they so wish.

It is true, as Bolton himself has pointed out on more than one occasion, that buying an index fund carries its own risks. When markets are running strongly on momentum, as happened for example in the latter stages of the bull market, index funds can be carried to dangerously high levels by their own self-reinforcing process – they buy shares only because they are already going up. In such markets, the ties to fundamental value become ever looser, and the risks of disappointing future performance increase as a result. At other times the reverse is true. There are occasions when the contrarian value-based investment approach that Bolton pursues has also become flavour of the month, and the case for investing in his fund becomes less attractive. As has been noted, the best time in the past to have bought his fund has been when its performance has been relatively poor (as it was in 1992 or 1998). It has not been when it has been exceptionally successful.

A further observation to be made is that it is worth looking carefully at the risk characteristics of funds that investors might be thinking of buying. Analysing risk in investment is a more complex, multi-faceted business than might at first appear to the casual observer. Historic volatility, the standard tool for measuring risk in investment, is a useful but blunt instrument. The wide array of statistical tools such as r-squared and information ratios that are now available to professional fund analysts are a valuable extension to the investor's armoury. But even they only capture one part of the risk that investors face. Investors need to look carefully at how funds have performed in different phases of the market cycle, as well as at such intangible factors as the character of any fund manager they choose.

---

[5] This is evidenced by the fact that Fidelity, the leading exponent of active management, now offers some index funds to its clients, while Vanguard, the leading indexing firm for private investors, also offers a range of actively managed funds to its clients.

The final point to make is that the world's financial markets are a tough and demanding environment in which to seek an enduring advantage. The real lesson of Anthony Bolton's success over the past 25 years is that beating the market, while a laudable ambition, is nowhere near as easy as it suits everyone in the financial services business to make it out to be. Devoting 25 years to the task, and drawing on the considerable resources and experience of the world's largest independent investment management firm, as Bolton has been able to do, has rightly earned him a reputation that is second to none in his professional peer group. Yet he is the first to concede that the biggest virtue any investor, however great, needs is humility. However clear it might appear in retrospect, he has never assumed that his success was inevitable. In that his attitude echoes the sentiments of other great investors down the years.

Appendices

What is in the appendices

1. Fidelity Special Situations: The 25-year record

(a) Analysis by Alastair MacDougall, Head of Research, WM Company

(b) Analysis by Lee Gardhouse, Fund of funds manager, Hargreaves Lansdown

2. Anthony Bolton's 10 largest holdings on an annual basis

3. Standard & Poor's ratings report on Fidelity Special Situations (October 2004)

4. Fidelity Special Values: analyst's report, Close Winterflood Securities (September 2004)

5. Fidelity's relationship with companies it invests in

6. An example of Fidelity's in-house research: William Hill (spring 2003)

7. Pages of the first managers report (October 1980)

1. Fidelity Special Situations: The 25-year record

(a) Analysis by Alastair MacDougall
Head of Research, WM Company

Introduction

In this discussion we use our perspective as performance measurers to analyse the performance characteristics of the Fidelity Special Situations Fund. The fund has been managed by Anthony Bolton since inception in December 1979.

In what follows we assess the fund performance with reference to its sector peer group (the 'All Companies' sector) and the FTSE All-Share Index (a broad market index of UK shares) in order to determine the level of performance of the fund and how the performance has been achieved.

What type of fund is it?

Fidelity note that the fund is managed more aggressively than most of their other UK funds, with the aim of providing investors with long-term capital growth. Bolton is a stockpicker, as opposed to following a more thematic investment approach. The fund is typically biased towards mid and small capitalised stocks. It is currently valued at around £3.5 billion and holds around 190 stocks.

How risky is it?

The decision to invest in equities exposes the investor to market risk. The next decision that needs to be taken is how much active risk to take? An investor who does not wish to take active risk will invest in a tracker fund, with the type of tracker being dependent on his definition of the market. All other investors will take active risk to varying degrees; the more aggressive the fund, the higher the active risk.

It is fairly obvious that once the decision to appoint an active manager is taken, the investor should be looking for truly active management as opposed to what is termed 'closet indexing', whereby the fund manager takes only modest bets relative to a market index but expects (and gets) active fees.

Given Fidelity's own description of the fund as 'aggressive', just how risky has it been over the years?

Market risk can be assessed by calculating a fund's absolute volatility, defined as the standard deviation of returns. In Chart 1 we show the absolute volatility of the Special Situations Fund and its peers over rolling three year periods from inception. The Special Situations Fund is shown as the heavy black line. The results of the peer group are shown as the grey coloured areas. The dark grey shaded area encompasses the 'inter-quartile' range of absolute risks – the middle 50% of the peer group. The lighter grey shaded area encompasses the 5th-95th percentile of absolute risks for the peer group. By comparing the dark line to the shaded areas, it is possible to establish how much risk the fund has taken relative to its peers.

Chart 1: Range of absolute risks over 3-year periods for trusts from UK All Companies sector

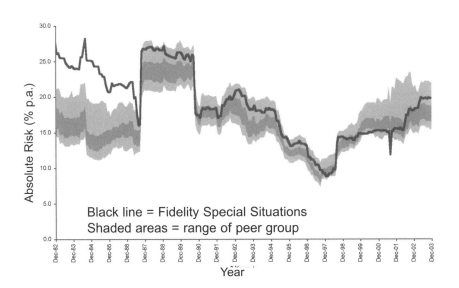

Apart from the earliest periods, when the fund's absolute risk was somewhat higher, the fund's absolute risk has been broadly similar to the other funds in the S&P All Companies sector.

In terms of active risk, the picture is very different however. The active risks shown in Chart 2 are defined as the standard deviations of the relative returns of the funds in the S&P All Companies sector. All the fund returns have been compared to the FTSE All-Share Index to provide the relative results.

Chart 2: Range of active risks over 3 year periods for trusts from UK All Companies sector

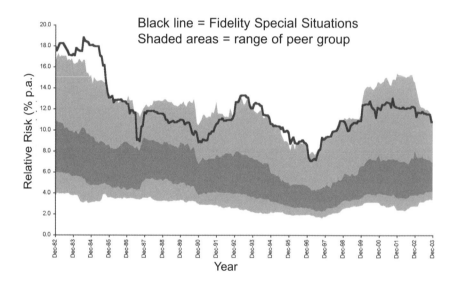

Over the entire period of management the Special Situations fund has consistently run risks relative to the index that are far higher than nearly all of its peers. Its average three-year active risk over the period since 1980 has been 11.9% p.a. The Special Situations fund has therefore been managed on a significantly different basis than most of its peer group. By definition, an All-Share tracker fund would run an active risk close to zero. As a result the fund would be expected to perform very differently (much better returns or much worse) than either most of its competitors or the market.

How does it invest?

Having established that the Special Situations fund has been quite a different animal to the great majority of its peers over its existence, we can use returns-based style analysis to provide greater insights into how Anthony Bolton has invested through time. Recall that Fidelity has characterised the fund as a bottom-up fund biased towards small and mid-sized UK stocks.

Returns-based style analysis uses a multiple regression approach to provide a strong indication of what a trust is invested in. It therefore provides a basis for comparing what the manager says he does and what he has done. The analysis decomposes the sources of a fund's performance using the combination of index returns that best represents that return. In other words the approach expresses a fund's performance as the return of a weighted average of sub-benchmarks underlying the broad market. In the analysis below we consider funds' investment styles in two dimensions, which can be captured very effectively within a 'style grid'.

In the style grids which follow, the vertical axes of the grids determine exposure to growth or value investing. The horizontal axes determine the extent to which a fund is biased towards or away from FTSE 100 stocks. The chart over the page is a style grid using the nine years of data from 1995 when the FTSE 350 High and Low Yield indices – proxies for growth and value investing were introduced – to 2003. There are no indices that allow us to infer the value/growth bias within the Fidelity fund's small company holdings but the High and Low Yield indices give us the ability to infer this for the fund's large and mid-sized holdings.

Chart 3: Style map of funds in UK All Companies sector 1995-2003

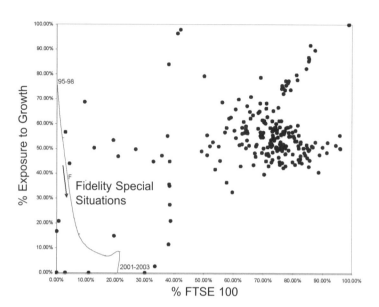

We show how the Fidelity Special Situations fund's style has changed through time using a 'snail trail' following the style through the seven rolling three-years periods that can be created from the nine year record. Over this period the fund has moved from a growth bias with no perceptible exposure to FTSE 100 stocks to a much more value based approach and a 20-25% exposure, to large capitalised stocks.[1]

The black dots on the chart represent the style points of the fund's 35 longest-lives competitor funds. The snail trails of the peer group funds have not been included in the grid to ease illustration but two aspects of the competition are worthy of note:

- The clustering of points indicates that many of these funds have maintained more consistent styles than has been the case for the Fidelity fund.

- The styles for the majority of the peer group centre around a broad market exposure to large stocks and a balanced exposure to growth/value – in other words, they look quite like the market. The Fidelity fund by comparison doesn't look anything like the market.

[1] It has to be noted that Anthony Bolton queries the 'growth bias' description, which he regards as misleading. (Author's note).

To boost the number of comparative funds, we repeated the style grid (Chart 4) but using only the last three years of data. This analysis therefore compares the Fidelity Fund against 220 peers. A number of similarly biased funds can be identified but the picture of many funds having a broadly market based approach remains – it is in this area of the style grid that 'closet trackers' lurk – an unappealing prospect for active investors.

Chart 4: Style map of funds in UK All Companies sector 2000-2003

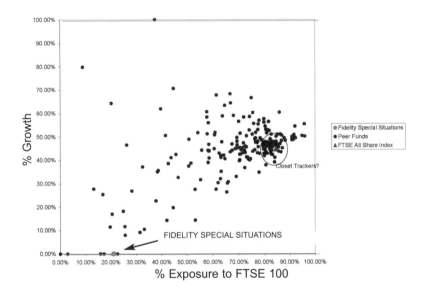

Style analysis is useful as it is extremely unlikely that a fund with a persistent style bias will exhibit consistent performance. Consistent outperformance is the holy grail of active management. Consistent good performance will only be available to investors who can react appropriately to changing market conditions.

Returns

Relative to the UK equity market, we have determined that the Fidelity Special Situations fund has been one of the riskiest given its style biases and high level of active management through time. The risks have been taken with a view to generating long-term capital growth for investors, significantly ahead of what could have been achieved by passive investing or other actively managed funds. How successful has the Fidelity Special Situation fund been?

In Chart 5, we show the growth in value of £100 invested in the Fidelity Special Situation fund since inception. We compare this to the same investment in the FTSE All-Share Index and the fund's long-term (35) competitors in the S&P All Companies sector.

Chart 5: £100 invested at the start of 1980

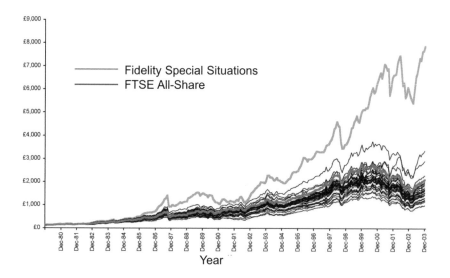

The outcome for the Fidelity fund is impressive. The £100 invested would have grown over the period to the end of 2003 to over £7,500, an annualised rate of return of 19.9% p.a. This compares to the market return of 13.5% p.a. Most of the competitor funds shown underperformed the market.

Of course, the use of cumulative performance figures can be highly distorting allowing fund managers (and unwary IFAs) to claim top quartile performance for a fund over, say, one, three, five and ten year periods due to isolated years of good performance.

Assessing performance over annual and rolling periods ensures that such 'blip' years do not distort the performance profile and has the further benefit of allowing the determination of performance trends (or cycles). Chart 6 shows the annual return of the Fidelity Special Situations Fund from 1980 to 2003, relative to the FTSE All-Share Index.

Chart 6: Return of Fidelity Special Situations relative to FTSE All-Share Index annually from 1980

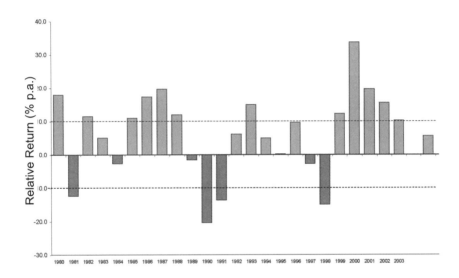

Of the full 24 years of calendar data shown, the fund outperformed in seventeen years. Earlier we stated that the risk profile of the fund would lead to the expectation of highly divergent performance from the market. This is borne out by the chart; in sixteen of the years shown the Fund outperformed or underperformed in excess of 10%.

Chart 7 shows the performance of the fund over rolling three-year periods, again relative to the FTSE All-Share Index and with the S&P 'All Companies' sector shown as a back-drop.

Chart 7: Relative Return spread over 3-year periods for trusts from UK All Companies sector

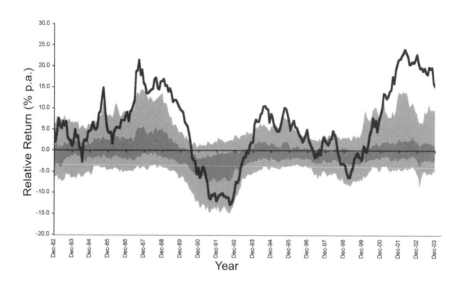

The Fidelity fund has been fairly consistently at the top end of performance. Relative performance over the most recent periods (including the bear market) has been particularly strong. The only significant period of poor relative returns in the Fidelity performance record occurred in the early 1990s.

Consistency and risk adjusted performance

Consistency of performance is a key element in successful active management. Investing in funds with a heavy style bias can lead to highly cyclical performance and to a natural (but misguided in our view) tendency to attempt to time switches from one fund to another.

As shown in Table 1, the performance of the Fidelity Special Situations fund has been highly consistent, in the top quartile of competitor funds in all discrete three-year periods with the exception of the period 1989-91.

Table 1: Consistency of funds discrete 3-year time periods

Year	Quartile	Rank	Year	Information ratio
1980-82	1	5th out of 58	1980-82	0.27
1983-85	1	8th out of 58	1983-85	0.33
1986-88	1	1st out of 94	1986-88	1.42
1989-91	4	87th out of 94	1989-91	-1.15
1992-94	1	3rd out of 154	1992-94	0.82
1995-97	1	12th out of 154	1995-97	0.25
1998-00	1	10th out of 128	1998.00	0.71
2001-03	1	2nd out of 128	2001-03	1.40

Source: WM Company

We have shown that the fund has historically been risky in relative terms but that this risk-taking has been rewarded by exceptionally strong and consistent performance. We can conflate the returns and risks relative to the market by means of a unitary measure of performance known as the information ratio. This measures the quality of the added value provided by active management. It is calculated by dividing the fund return in excess/deficit of the FTSE All-Share Index by the fund's active risk. An information ratio of 1 therefore means that each 1% of active risk is converted to 1% of excess return.

The ratio is often interpreted as a measure of manager skill as it assesses the extent to which active risk is converted into excess return. The higher the information ratio, the more skilful the manager is perceived to be. In Table 2 we show the information ratio of the Fidelity Special Situations fund over the same discrete three-year periods as Table 1.

The Information Ratio for the fund has varied widely over the periods shown. In order to provide some context to the ratios shown, it should be noted that:

- For the average professionally managed fund in the market, information ratio is negative after costs because, in aggregate, managers can only achieve the market index performance, from which their fees are deducted.

- Institutional managers with good recent performance will advertise an information ratio of 0.5 with satisfaction.

Conclusions

As fund manager, Anthony Bolton has achieved very significant, and consistent, outperformance since the inception of the fund by following a highly active investment approach, significantly at odds with most other funds within the S&P All Companies sector. This is an impressive achievement given that the asset size is now well above £3.5 billion and the fund contains almost 200 holdings.

Two main obstacles would appear to conspire against a continuation of this performance. Firstly, can outperformance continue as the fund's asset base grows, particularly if the focus on predominately UK shares remain? Secondly, as the fund is so associated with Anthony Bolton, how likely is it that a successor could maintain the level of performance generated into the future?

(b) Analysis by Lee Gardhouse
Fund of funds manager, Hargreaves Lansdown

Our general approach

Our approach is to measure the performance of all the funds we look to invest in, or recommend to our clients, against a range of different style indicators. The computer program is one that we have developed in-house and we find provides us with a valuable tool for distinguishing between those managers whose funds do well when and if their particular style of investing is also working well and those who are genuinely adding value through their stock selection. Both types of fund can have their uses – a fund that tracks a consistent market style may be valuable at times – but finding a manager with proven and sustainable stockpicking ability is what really interests us, as they are rare beasts.

For funds in the UK All Companies sector, of which Fidelity Special Situations is one, we look at the capital return from the FTSE All-Share Index and similar monthly data for a number of style indices. The programme tells us how much the fund would be expected to have returned given its exposure to certain well-known style factors, such as market capitalisation and 'value' versus 'growth' (using as a proxy in the latter case the relative performance of high and low yielding stocks). We then look at how the actual return for Fidelity Special Situations compares with what would be expected on style grounds. As a rough approximation, the difference between the two returns can be attributed to the stockpicking skill of the fund manager.

The stockpicking series we calculate for any fund we look at comes from taking the monthly differential between the expected and actual return and compounding it over time. Because the relevant data did not start appearing until 1986, we are unable to analyse the performance of the fund all the way back to its origins in 1979. Our analysis begins in 1990 by when we have four years of data for the FTSE value and growth indices.

Chart 1: Style analysis of Fidelity Special Situations 1990-2004

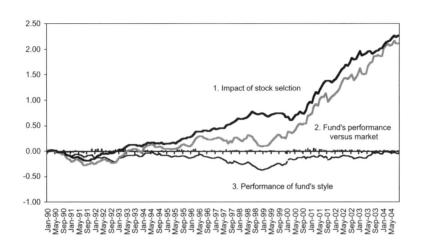

What the charts show

The charts summarise how Fidelity Special Situations has performed when measured against two of the style benchmarks our programme has developed. The first one, dubbed simply 'style' for shorthand, compares the fund's actual performance to an index based on a mixture of style and size factors. The second one, 'size' for short, measures its performance against an index based solely on size (market capitalisation).

In each chart, the bottom line tracks the performance of the fund's expected return, given its style and size exposure, against that of the market, as represented by the FTSE All-Share Index. When the line is falling, it means that the style is underperforming the market. When it is rising, the reverse is true. The other two lines show the cumulative outperformance of the market that Fidelity Special Situations has achieved; and the contribution to this outperformance made by Anthony Bolton's stockpicking abilities. As can be seen, in both cases, over the whole period since 1990 stockpicking has accounted for all (or nearly all) of the fund's outperformance.

Taking the style chart first, it shows how the style of the fund, which in general is biased towards value and small and midcap stocks, has performed in the fourteen years since the series began. The style of the fund largely worked against performance in the period 1990-1992 (a very poor period for small and midcap stocks) and again from 1996 to 1999 (when large cap and growth stocks were both much in demand). At other times, and in particular from 1999 onwards, the style of the fund has tended to work strongly in its favour.

Over the whole period 1990-2004, however, the style effects largely cancel each other out. In other words, a fund manager who purely followed that style for the past fourteen years without demonstrating any stockpicking ability would have performed almost exactly in-line with the FTSE All-Share Index. In fact, the fund has done markedly better than the index over the period, indicating how important Anthony Bolton's stockpicking has been to its performance.

Chart 2: Size analysis of Fidelity Special Situations 1990-2004

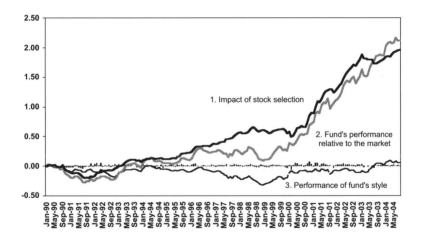

A similar picture emerges from the size-only style analysis. The chart shows the way that small and midcap stocks fell increasingly out of favour in the period to 1999, but have since rebounded strongly. In the early period under review, the fund had a particularly large exposure to small cap stocks. Midcap stocks begin to play a more prominent part from 1993 onwards.

Today more than 70% of the exposure is in midcap orientated stocks. This may obviously be connected to the fact that the size of the fund has increased so dramatically in recent years. The size bias of the Special Situations fund inevitably dragged down its performance in the later years of the 1990s, when large capitalisation stocks dominated the stock market performance tables.

This was offset to some extent by the impact of superior stockpicking. Since 1999, the combination of a renewed style tailwind and continued stockpicking ability has contributed to the fund's massive outperformance of the market. Once again we can see that the fund should have performed broadly in line with that of the index over the period purely on style grounds. That it has in fact outperformed significantly can be put down to strong stock selection.

Chart 3: Percentile ranking of the fund 1990-2004

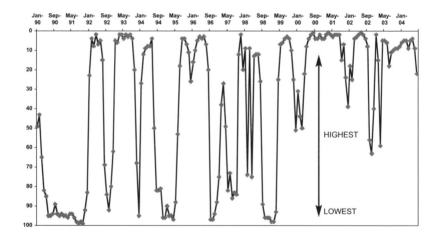

Another interesting perspective on the fund's performance is the consistency of its performance against its peer group. The chart summarises the rolling six-month percentile ranking that the fund has achieved over the period since January 1990. At the beginning, on a rolling six-month basis the fund was pretty much the worst fund in its peer group for over a year. This was followed by some extreme volatility of performance versus the peer group until the end of 1998. Since then the fund has consistently been placed at the top of its peer group.

Our data says that stock selection, our measure of the contribution made by stockpicking skills, has been greater than zero in 71% of the months covered. In our experience, a positive return from stockpicking is significant when it happens in more than 60% of months. Stock selection has contributed more than 2% to the fund's monthly performance in one in four of the months covered by our analysis, and had a negative impact of more than 2% in only one in twenty. In other words, stock selection has not only been consistently good, but has provided few nasty surprises.

On both counts the fund's record stacks up very strongly against most of its competitors. The net stock selection return, our measure of how much value has been added by the manager per month through stock selection, has been 1.66% per month. We view any figure of above 0.5% as being substantial and significant. The 1.66% figure achieved by the Special Situations fund compounds to about 20% a year and is once again exceptional for the sector.

Conclusion

As with the majority of managers, the style of Fidelity Special Situations does not change that much. What has driven performance is the success of Anthony Bolton's stock selection, not his style. Great investor though he is, he is no better than anyone else at predicting changes in style, that is when value is going to take over from growth, or when the small/midcap sector of the market is going to do better than large cap stocks.

Over the period since 1990, our quantitative assessment shows that Anthony Bolton has done an extremely impressive job of picking the right companies in his investment arena. The consistency of his stockpicking return is unrivalled in duration and magnitude for the period that we are covering.

2. Anthony Bolton's 10 largest holdings on an annual basis

1981	%	1982	%	1983	%
Pleasurama	4.5	ICL	7.4	Pleasurama	6.0
Westland	3.7	Petrocon	5.9	ICL	5.9
Barker & Dobson	3.4	Moben	5.7	Moben	4.6
British Land	3.3	Pleasurama	5.0	Woolworth	4.5
Norgas	3.2	London & Liverpool Trust	4.7	Manchester Ship Canal	4.4
Town & City	3.2	Graig Shipping	3.6	Blackwood Hodge	4.1
Tunnel Holdings	3.1	L Ryan	3.5	CASE	3.8
Bowater	2.9	Standard Ind	3.3	FNFC	3.6
Reardon Smith	2.8	Hampton Trust	3.3	Lee Cooper	3.4
Moben	2.6	Barker & Dobson	3.0	L Ryan	3.2

1984	%	1985	%	1986	%
Bell Resources Opts	5.2	British Telecom	5.3	Montedison	4.7
Trident TV	4.7	Grattan	4.7	FNFC	4.0
Mersey Docks	4.3	Avon Rubber	4.4	Bernard Matthews	3.8
Armstrong Equipment	4.0	Hestair	4.4	Hestair	3.8
Lee Cooper	3.9	Actinor	4.2	Lucas	3.8
Norgas	3.9	FNFC	4.2	Johnson Firth Brown	3.8
L Texas Pet	3.5	Lucas Industries	3.2	Raybeck	3.3
Tozer Kemsley	3.3	Ganger Rolf	3.0	Hewden-Stuart	3.1
Vitatron	3.2	Lee Cooper	2.7	Grattan	2.8
FNFC	3.0	Hogg Robinson	2.7	Aurora	2.6

1987	%	1988	%	1989	1%
VSEL	3.9	Hafslund	4.0	Security Services/ Securicor	6.4
Chloride	3.6	Mersey Docks	3.8	Magnet	3.5
Security Services	3.5	Security Services/ Securicor	3.6	British Aerospace	3.5
Polly Peck	3.5	Torras Hostench	3.3	Lloyds Bank	3.3
Magnet & Southerns	3.2	Atlantic Computers	3.2	LWT	3.2
Apricot Computers	3.2	Rothmans	3.2	TV-am	2.6
Thames TV	3.0	Polly Peck	3.1	Ultramar	2.4
Hawley Group	3.0	Magnet	2.9	Polly Peck	2.3
Hestair	2.5	Midland Bank	2.8	VSEL	2.2
Debron Investments	2.5	Ultramar	2.7	Elkem	2.1

1990	%	1991	%	1992	%
Security Services/ Securicor	4.6	Colonia	4.6	Granada	3.8
Abbey National	4.0	Abbey National	3.8	Wickes	3.6
Ashley Group	2.7	Ashley Group	3.4	BAA	3.6
Ultramar	2.6	De La Rue	3.0	Security Services/ Securicor	3.3
Colonia	2.6	Rothmans	2.7	St James's Place	3.0
Parkfield	2.5	Telefonos de Mexico	2.5	Midland Bank	2.9
Lloyds Bank	2.3	VSEL	2.2	Wessex Water	2.8
Telefonos de Mexico	2.1	Eurotunnel	2.1	Scottish TV	2.6
Rothmans	2.1	Suter	2.1	LWT	2.5
Barclays Bank	2.1	Western Company of North America	1.9	Central TV	2.5

1993	%	1994	%	1995	%
Security Services/ Securicor	5.7	Security Services/ Securicor	5.6	Security Services/ Securicor	5.4
News International	3.6	Wickes	3.0	London International Group	3.1
Wessex Water	3.5	WPP	2.8	FNFC	2.7
Wickes	3.4	Mirror Group Newspapers	2.7	Wickes	2.5
Oriflame International	3.2	News International	2.6	Tesco	2.4
Burton	3.1	FNFC	2.5	News International	2.4
VSEL	3.1	Anglia TV	2.3	London Clubs International	2.4
Biochem Pharmaceutical	3.1	Crockfords	2.3	Berisford International	2.3
WPP	3.0	ACT	2.2	Biochem Pharmaceutical	2.2
St James's Place Capital	3.0	Tesco	2.2	WPP Group	2.1

1996	%	1997	%	1998	%
Security Services/ Securicor	4.5	LIMIT	2.7	LIMIT	3.2
Wickes	3.8	Berisford	2.4	Berisford	3.1
T&N	2.6	Misys	2.2	Oriflame International	2.6
London Clubs International	2.4	Wembley	2.1	Somerfield	2.6
News International	2.4	Man ED & F	2.1	Man ED & F	2.5
Oriflame International	2.3	Micro Focus	2.0	Micro Focus	2.4
Misys	2.3	Oriflame International	1.9	Misys	2.1
Psion	2.2	T&N	1.9	Wembley	1.7
Berisford	2.1	APV	1.7	De La Rue	1.7
Mirror Group Newspapers	2.0	WPP	1.6	Hazlewood Foods	1.5

1999	%	2000	%	2001	%
Berisford	3.2	Celltech Chiroscience	2.0	Bank of Ireland	2.7
LIMIT	2.9	Johnson Matthey	2.0	Reed International	2.1
Man ED & F	2.4	LIMIT	1.9	BAA	2.1
De La Rue	2.4	Cadiz	1.7	Gallaher	2.0
Reuters	2.3	Berisford	1.7	British Energy	2.0
Iceland Group	2.2	Safeway	1.7	Safeway	1.9
Wembley	1.9	De La Rue	1.6	Novar	1.9
Hogg Robinson	1.8	Autonomy	1.6	Royal & Sun Alliance	1.9
Kewill Systems	1.7	Wembley	1.6	Carillion	1.8
London Clubs Int	1.6	Booker	1.6	Garban-Intercapital	1.8

2002	%	2003	%
Bank of Ireland	2.1	Safeway	4.3
Unilever	2.0	Amlin	2.4
Safeway	1.9	MMO2	2.3
Credit Lyonnais	1.9	Unilever	2.2
Enterprise Oil	1.9	Wellington Underwriting	1.8
Wimpey George	1.9	Cable & Wireless	1.7
London Stock Exchange	1.9	SSL International	1.6
Gallaher	1.9	Provident Financial	1.6
Carlton	1.8	Somerfield	1.6
British Energy	1.6	Prudential	1.5

Notes for tables of largest holdings

1. % = percentage of fund assets

2. Dates of valuations:

1981	1 May
1982	5 September
1983	14 March
1984	5 March
1985	12 March
1986	21 March
1987	23 March
1988 - 1998	5 March
1999 - 2003	28 February

3. Standard & Poor's ratings report on Fidelity Special Situations (October 2004)

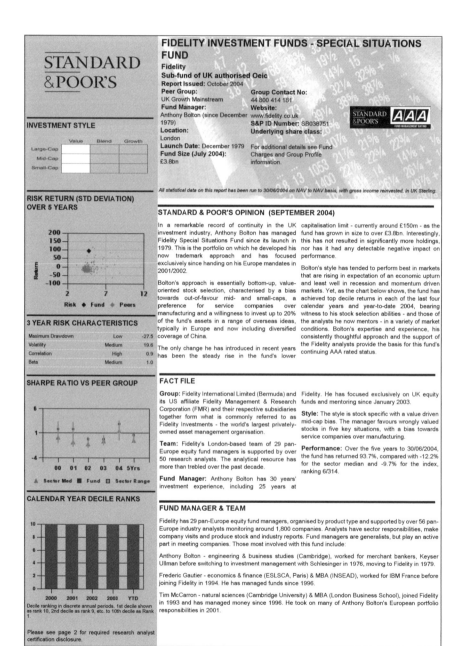

PORTFOLIO CHARACTERISTICS

No. of holdings	190
Turnover ratio (%)	56
% in top 10	24

TOP 10 HOLDINGS (01/07/04)

	%
BP	4.2
ITV	2.9
Cairn Energy	2.5
Shell	2.4
MMO2 *	2.3
Standard Chartered	2.0
BG	1.9
Hilton	1.9
Prudential *	1.9
Allied Irish Banks	1.8

* In top 10 holdings a year ago

ALLOCATION BREAKDOWN (01/07/04)

	Index %**	Fund %
Basic Industries	4	4
Cyclical Consumer Goods	-	-
Cyclical Services	15	29
Financials	28	26
General Industrials	2	3
Investment Trusts	-	-
Non-Cyclical Consumer Goods	18	9
Non-Cyclical Services	11	5
Resources	17	16
Technology	1	2
Utilities	4	-
Other	-	3
Cash	-	3

PERFORMANCE STATISTICS

	3 Years	5 Years
Fund	25.3%	93.7%
Standard & Poor's Peer Median	-12.5%	-12.2%
Index	-7.9%	-9.7%
Fund Rank	7/380	6/314
Standard Deviation	19.6	-
Relative Standard Deviation	1.2	-
Volatility Adjusted Ranking	6/380	-

CUMULATIVE PERFORMANCE

- FTSE All Share (xd adj) — Fund
- UK Growth Mainstream

FIDELITY INVESTMENT FUNDS - SPECIAL SITUATIONS FUND

Peer Group: UK Growth Mainstream

STANDARD & POOR'S AAA FUND MANAGEMENT RATING

MANAGEMENT STYLE

• Bolton's management style has evolved over the last 25 years with this fund into a stock specific, value-driven approach, with a strong bias towards mid-caps. Larger companies are held, but those capitalised below £150m are often considered too illiquid or just too small for this near £4bn portfolio.

• Mis-valued stocks are targeted in five broad categories - recovery situations, discount to assets, industry anomalies, unrecognised growth and corporate potential - only the balance of which changes over time. Service companies are preferred over manufacturing.

• Although benchmarked against the FTSE All Share index, up to 20% of assets are typically invested overseas - currently a mix of Europe and China - and reflected most noticeably in long-held exposure to Scandinavia.

• Bolton is aided by input from the group's analysts, but he also acts as mentor to some of the team, passing on the benefit of his long experience. He looks for unconventional ideas and is prepared to buy early on bad news.

• An initial stake is usually around 25bps, which can then be raised on further conviction, leading to a fully invested portfolio of around 200 names.

• The manager does not use derivatives.

PORTFOLIO REVIEW

The fund has doubled in size over the last 12 months to over £3.8bn, causing Bolton to emphasise mid-250 stocks - now 35% of assets - at the expense of FTSE Smallcap names, now under 11%.

This move up the cap scale was also a function of the better value being found in mid- and large-caps, with the fund's FTSE 100 exposure rising from 20% to over 35%. Purchases included Prudential, Aviva, Shell and BP, the latter now the largest position in the portfolio, although at 4.2% it is still 3.8% under index weight. The overall number of holdings held at around 190.

The fund had no exposure to banks other than Standard Chartered and Abbey. It was also out of Vodafone and Glaxo.

Overseas exposure (18%) has focused on Europe and a range of China plays gaining diversified exposure to the domestic market via Hong Kong and through "A" shares in instruments offered by UBS.

Developing themes included gambling (Hilton and William Hill), property and mature PFI projects in hospitals and schools.

PERFORMANCE ANALYSIS (JULY 2004)

The fund has produced top decile relative returns in each of the last four calendar years, creating one of the strongest track records in its sector. The last time performance slipped out of top quartile was in the highly momentum driven market of 1998-99.

Longer term performance is also very strong and demonstrates the success of Bolton's contrarian/value style which tends to produce the best relative returns in steadily rising markets and does least well in periods of recession and in strong momentum markets. Bolton's definition of value is very broad encompassing some growth companies that may be undervalued compared to M&A valuations.

Success over the last 12 months came from a strong bias to insurance and property, good stock selection in the oil and resource sectors and by running double-weight coverage of the cyclical service sectors.

Notable individual stock successes were Cairn Energy, Carlton (media), Hilton Group (bookmakers) and Pendragon (car distributors).

DISCRETE PERFORMANCE (CALENDAR YEARS)

	2000		2001		2002		2003		YTD 30/06/2004	
	%	Rank	%	Rank	%	Rank	%	Rank	%	Rank
Fund	26.1	7/331	3.8	10/365	-10.5	7/415	33.5	39/484	11.7	15/500
Index**	-5.4		-12.7		-22.1		21.9		3.3	
Median	-3.9		-13.3		-23.7		20.1		3	

** FTSE All Share (xd adj) (Source: FTSE International)

The McGraw-Hill Companies

4. Fidelity Special Values: analyst's report, Close Winterflood Securities (September 2004)

Close WINS Investment Trusts   *22 October 2004*

Fidelity Special Values plc

UK- Growth Sector

☐   **Anthony Bolton runs this fund on a bottom-up, stock-picking basis with an emphasis on under-valued companies.**

☐   **This is not a mainstream UK fund as the portfolio is heavily biased towards Mid and Small Cap stocks (45% of the portfolio), and in addition, 19% is invested overseas including 13% in Continental European stocks and small allocations to investments in China, Hong Kong and USA.**

☐   **Performance has been extremely strong through different market conditions and the NAV has increased by 106% over a five-year period compared to a decline of 5% for the fund's benchmark, the FTSE All-Share.**

☐   **Anthony Bolton is regarded highly, but while this fund is trading at a premium, the obvious alternative is the equivalent open-ended fund, which offers an almost identical portfolio other than the gearing.**

■ Management

Experienced & high profile manager

Since its launch in 1994, this fund has been managed by Anthony Bolton, an experienced and high profile fund manager who has been with Fidelity for nearly 25 years. He previously also ran Fidelity European Values and other continental European money but over the past couple of years has reduced his commitments and now focuses solely on predominantly UK orientated funds. He still runs Fidelity Special Situations Fund (£4bn), which is managed on an identical basis. Anthony Bolton has stated that he will continue to manage to at least to the beginning of 2005 and currently believes that his involvement will be for longer.

■ Investment Process & Portfolio

Mid & Small Cap bias

The manager's focus is on mis-valued securities with a bias towards stocks in the mid and small cap. He will only invest in companies with market caps over £100m. The portfolio is not managed relative to its benchmark, the FTSE All-Share, and sector weightings are the result of stock selection. He is willing to adopt a contrarian approach and buy unfashionable companies.

Anthony Bolton has become more active as a shareholder in recent years because he sees it as a method of increasing an investment's value. As a result, Fidelity now employs a corporate financier to co-ordinate shareholders in such actions.

Portfolio Sector Breakdown

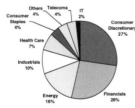

Source: Close WINS, The Company as at 31 August 2004

Portfolio weighting vs. Benchmark Constituents

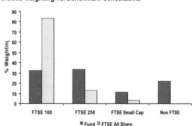

Source: Close WINS, The Company as at 30 September 2004

19% of portfolio invested overseas

The fund can invest up to 20% of its portfolio in non-UK investments and, at present, 19% of the portfolio is invested overseas including 13% in continental European stocks. Although Anthony Bolton no longer runs dedicated European mandates, he still takes a close interest in the region and attends selected company meetings. In the past year, small allocations have also been made to investments in China (1.7% of the portfolio), Hong Kong (1.4%) and the USA (1.8%).

Close WINS Investment Trusts *22 October 2004*

Gearing

Gearing is currently 16% of net assets and consists of fixed rate debt, the majority of which has been borrowed on a short-term basis. The Board has set the fund's maximum gearing at 25%.

■ Performance

Consistently strong performance

The fund has achieved strong, consistent performance through very different market conditions over the last five years. However, the manager believes that his style suits certain markets better than others and he does not generally expect incremental quarter-by-quarter out-performance but rather "lumpy" results. For instance, he believes the fund, with its mid-cap bias, may under-perform in recessions, when smaller more domestically exposed businesses find conditions the hardest.

Alternatively, the fund, with its value orientation, should not perform well in momentum driven markets such as those in 1997/98 and the mid 80s, although performance was good in 1999 due to the level of corporate activity and favourable sector themes.

5 Year NAV Relative Performance

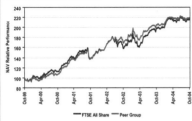

— FTSE All Share — Peer Group

Source: Close WINS, Thomson Financial Datastream

5 Year Discount History

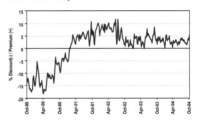

Source: Close WINS, Thomson Financial Datastream

■ Discount History

New issues issued regularly to meet demand

In early 1999, the fund was trading on a 20% discount, but strong NAV performance led to a sharp rerating and it has traded at a premium over the past three years. The fund is largely owned by private clients and new shares have regularly been issued to meet demand, reflecting limited liquidity in the secondary market. So far this year, nearly 2.4m shares have been issued.

The fund's premium rating and strong track record has allowed its participation in corporate activity. At the end of 2003, 12.1m shares were issued in exchange for £39m of assets resulting from the reconstruction of two investment trusts, Go vett Strategic and Derby Trust. The fund also saw over 3m shares issued in January this year, following the expiry of its remaining warrants.

■ Close WINS View

Obvious alternative is equivalent open-ended fund

This fund benefits from experienced management that has delivered an impressive long-term performance record through varying market conditions. However, this is not a mainstream UK fund and while it is trading at a premium, the obvious alternative is the equivalent open-ended fund, Fidelity Special Situations, which is also managed by Anthony Bolton and offers an almost identical portfolio other than the gearing.

5. Fidelity's relationship with companies it invests in

In July 2004 Anthony Bolton gave an interview to *Real IR*, a monthly magazine about investor relations in Europe, in which he discussed the way that Fidelity conducts its relationships with companies it invests in and gave his views on a number of current corporate governance issues. The article is reproduced here with the permission of Caspian Publishing, the magazine's publishers (www.realir.net for more information).

Meeting companies

Our main relationship with companies is one-to-one meetings with executive management. Our Pan-European team had 2,600 routine meetings last year. I don't think there's anyone else who has as much contact with companies, and we like to think that we are demanding, fair and professional in our requests for information. In addition to these routine meetings, we also as a group held about 120 meetings with companies which were of a corporate governance nature. These were normally meetings with chairmen, non-exec directors or advisors to companies.

The meetings fall into two types. The majority are ones instigated by the company or its financial advisers. The second type are ones where we or a third party have sought the meeting. The first meetings typically come about when companies are considering making an important decision affecting the direction of the company, and we as large shareholders would expect to be consulted. We like to be involved in major decisions.

Examples would be strategic decisions about the direction of the company, a major acquisition, major board changes, incentives and remuneration schemes, things of that sort. We always try and vote our shares wherever possible, and we like to have that direct discussion when a company is going to make a change. We feel that's part of being a responsible shareholder. Where we're asked for feedback, and we've got a view – we don't always have a view – we will give it.

Seeking change

The second type of meeting is rarer, but has the potential to be more headline-making. Most of the time we're happy with the companies we're invested in, but in a smaller number of companies – and they're nearly always the underperforming ones – as an alternative to selling out what we might do on occasions is try to change what's happening at the company. Generally we're not trying to change the way companies are run, so it's the exception rather than the rule. We nearly always act in cases of this sort in conjunction with other big shareholders. Usually we've talked to two or three of the other big shareholders who have a similar view.

There were about 50 cases last year where we intervened and acted as some sort of catalyst for change. To do that can be very time consuming, so you need an infrastructure. We decided a while back that it wasn't ideal for the fund managers to spend lots of their time doing this. We recruited a Corporate Finance Director a couple of years ago who's now the spearhead to this activity. He can sit behind a Chinese wall and is able to take price-sensitive information without tainting the whole of Fidelity. Often he'll then decide to bring the whole organisation inside the wall, but it is his responsibility, not the fund managers'.

The rationale for activism

The primary motivation is self-interest. Our investment style biases us towards midcap and larger small cap segments of the market. We're often amongst the two or three largest holders in these companies. Moving in and out of the stock can take time and be costly. So, where a company begins to underperform, and we think as a large shareholder that there's something obvious that needs to be changed for the better, as an alternative to saying "we don't agree with what's going on, let's sell the shares", our attitude is: why not move to change it? We think that's in the interest of all shareholders. At the same time, some of our institutional clients are now asking us to become more active. We also have the feeling that the Government and regulators would like us as institutional shareholders in general to take a more pro-active line.

On the ITV merger

The most important thing to say is to say is what happened with the Granada-Carlton merger was totally untypical of what we do. First of all, 99% of what we do is done in private behind closed doors. We think that's the best way to do it. Normally we won't speak to the press on this kind of issue. We only spoke to the press about the ITV business when it had already come out. We did it to give our side of the story, to balance the views. The other thing which was extremely unusual is that all this was identified with one person at Fidelity. That is not at all our style. It only came out because unfortunately one of the people whose views we'd canvassed, and whom I'd spoken to last summer, leaked it to the press. That is how it got identified with me personally.

On corporate governance in general

The general point to make is that we tend to be pragmatic rather than box tickers. We're not somebody who says "these are the rules and you must put a tick in every box". I fear some people think the box tick is more important than the overall view. What we are keen on is the chairman being a non-executive director and not the former CEO. We think quite a few of the problems that have come up have been where that's happened. We also like the use of share buybacks. If a company is going to make an acquisition, for example, our view is that it should test this option against the alternative of buying back its own shares. This and our other principles are all set out in a document we published last year.

How often is your intervention successful?

I don't think I could say precisely how many of the 50 cases where we intervened were successful. I would say it was the majority. It is often not that clear-cut. There was a company that came to us with a new share incentive programme last year which we thought was far too generous to the executives concerned. We gave that feedback to the company, they then went to two or three other shareholders who gave them a similar view and the end result was they dropped it. That sort of thing never comes out in public. It was kept quiet and that's the ideal way, from our perspective.

We're not trying to make detailed decisions. It has to be something pretty fundamental for us to want to be involved. Suppose a company has three main areas of business, one of which is not producing as good returns as the others. Should they stay in that business or not? Should they go into France or Germany next? We are not concerned about the detail, but the strategic issue. If we thought a company might command a higher valuation if it was split into two than if it stayed as one entity, we would want to have that type of argument.

Another example of where we got involved was where a company brought in a new CEO. He had a new plan for the business, but though it sounded as if it was going to do well, it was not producing results after a couple of years. We gave them our view that the best thing would be for them to put the business up for sale, which they subsequently did. I don't think we got thanked for it!

When do you like to get involved in this kind of decision?

We like to feel that we can do it at any time. You wouldn't want to pre-empt things if you knew a strategic review is coming up and a company is planning to announce it at the time of the results. You don't rush in before the results come up. I suppose it's natural for these kinds of meetings to take place in closed periods or just before the results.

On executive pay

I think some people in the Government would like to feel that we can adjudicate on the absolute levels of pay. I think that is very difficult. What we're much more concerned to do is avoid payment for failure. It is important for pay to be linked to success on the basis of guidelines which don't just reward people if the stock market goes up in the short term, but which ensure that the long term success of the business and the level of executive pay are linked together.

Should fund managers have to disclose their own remuneration?

I don't see why just because people [such as Sir John Banham] who have chosen to be in an industry where pay is made public should be entitled to ask for those in an industry where the pay is private to do the same. This is only my personal view. In general we want people to be well paid when they do well. People running companies should be paid highly for that responsibility. Our job is just to try and get the parameters right, so that they don't also do very well when the shareholders do very poorly.

How well do UK companies manage their investor relations?

I would say that in the UK, it's very rare for us to have a problem with information flow and communication. On the Continent that can still be the case, though it's changing there too. In some countries you find it [the problem of lack of information] more than in others. For a long time, the biggest company in Denmark wouldn't see shareholders, but it's changing even there.

How valuable is good IR to a company?

Good IR is a very useful asset. The majority of our meetings are with the CEO or Finance Director, or both. If an IR is well in the information loop and is given the authority to discuss issues and give direct answers to questions, then a meeting with them can be extremely useful. One specific example – in our system, analysts change sectors every 2-3 years, and it means that we have new analysts all the time who need to get up to speed on companies, to understand what it does, how it works, etc. That job is clearly not the best use of a CEO's time. A long meeting with the investor relations team is very helpful for that type of thing. At the other end of the scale, there was an Italian company that had a very good looking lady who knew nothing about the business and would answer no questions. That is useless.

How could IR practice be improved?

One of the things we've asked for, and this has become more common, is for synopses of meetings with investors, when a company does a road show or a round of meetings with various investors, should go to the whole board, including non-exec directors. If it goes through the hands of the executive directors on the way, our experience is that it can lose something in the translation! Often, the way it's done, the shareholders tell the advisors, the the advisors race off to tell the execs, but the non-execs are not always kept in the loop.

We like to give most of our feedback directly wherever possible rather than through an intermediary. There are times where maybe the message is something a company doesn't want to hear where the advisor can play a very good role. We have got a slightly complicated system in the UK, where you often have both an investment bank and the company broker involved. That can sometimes muddy the waters.

On presentations

A lot of companies now put these on their websites, which is welcome. When it comes to presentations, we normally like to use the presentation to have the company answer our analysts' questions, not to go through the whole presentation again. We like to hear whether there are things we have missed or other points that the company wants to make. What we don't find is best is if the company sets the whole agenda. They tend to gloss over the bits that we often want to talk about, and only talk about the good bits.

What I value highly is an open dialogue where companies are very happy to talk about the good things as well as the bad things, and they don't put spin and hype on it. In fact, I quite like people who underplay their hand rather than always than telling you it's going to be wonderful and then failing to deliver.

What lessons can be learnt from the recent Shell debacle?

Shell is a very complicated subject. It's got a very complex board structure. My observation would be that they are a very inward looking company, where the non-exec part of the board has very little influence on the company. I think Shell shows the risks of that kind of approach when things go wrong, when you don't have people cross-checking and outside people looking at the company. You could say they should have a non-exec chairman, but as they have a dual board structure, it is not as simple as that at Shell because of the Anglo-Dutch composition and dual boards. In general I prefer a single structure. I'm not saying that dual boards can't work but the supervisory board has to have enough input over the Exec board to be able to cross-examine them and expect reasonable replies.

Is it right that there is a shortage of suitably qualified non-exec directors?

Yes, that is one of my personal worries. There has to be decent pay for the job. However, I have to say that I asked a chairman of a large insurance company the same questions the other day – but he disputed that all the problems and scandals were making people less inclined to be non-execs. Our policy is that we never put specific people on boards of listed companies, just to represent Fidelity. We might however be in a group that puts someone up to represent all the institutional shareholders, not just us.

6. An example of Fidelity's in-house research: William Hill (spring 2003)

When picking stocks, Anthony Bolton can draw on the research of more than 50 analyst colleagues at Fidelity. The following pages provide an illustration of the in-depth analysis that emerges from the company's research process. The example chosen is William Hill, the bookmaking company that was floated on the stock market in June 2002. Bolton bought some shares around the time of the initial public offering, and added substantially to his holding in the course of 2003. The in-house analyst's report on the company at the time (when the shares were 227p) is shown on the next two pages. This is followed by the analyst's spreadsheet on the company. Fidelity's research process also produces a number of annexes that model different aspects of the company's operations (not shown here). Fidelity operates a ranking system that rates companies on the following scale: 1 strong buy 2 buy 3 hold 4 sell 5 strong sell.

Analysis is one thing, but the judgement call whether to buy the shares remains Bolton's own. He summed up his feelings about William Hill as follows:

"I don't normally buy a lot of shares in initial pubic offerings, because they tend to be priced for the seller, not the buyer. However William Hill was an exception. At the time of the flotation, it was perceived as a stable but rather dull business. It was the kind of business that I liked however, being cash generative and with a decent franchise. What made me decide to buy the shares in much greater volume in 2003 however was the realisation that fixed odds betting terminals had the potential to transform the economics of the business. I remember meeting a top executive from one of the bookmaking companies who told me that they were the most important development the industry had seen in the whole of his time in the business. That certainly made me sit up and take notice. We bought the shares on that basis. They are a good example of the 'unrecognised growth' that is one of my main investment themes. There was also the fact that the whole business of online gambling seemed to be taking off. There was still a good deal of uncertainty at the time, mainly because of the perceived regulatory risk involved. I took the view however that the scale of the potential business justified the risks involved. The rating of the shares did not fully discount the upside potential of the business".

London	Investment Report	**FT:** LEISURE & HOTELS **MSSP:** HOTELS RESTAURANTS & LEISURE
Rating: 1 (2) **Current Share Price: (UK PENCE) 227.000**		**WILLIAM HILL PLC (*WLHL)** **Company Market Cap: US$1,495M** SHAH, PARUS (8-727-4354)

- *More positive on horse betting mgns + FOBTs - Upgrading to a 1*

UNITED KINGDOM — Exchange Rate From USD to UK POUND: 0.64					Close of Business: Apr/2/2003	
Shares Outstanding (in Millions)	421.8		Percent of FT ALLSHARE (U.K.)			0.09%
Free Float	--%		Percent of MSCI EUROPE			0.00
Current Dividend Yield	3.9		Percent Owned / Allowed			
Book Value Per Share	59.30		Shares Available (in Millions)			9.7
Price/Book Value	3.83		Long-Term Debt to Total Capital			82.5%
Fiscal Year Ending Jan 31	**2001A**	**2002A**	**2003E**	**2004E**	**2005E**	**Q4 / 2003E**
Sales (in Millions)	2,452.0	3,365.0	4,467.0	4,967.0	5,326.0	--
Revenue Growth	--%	37.2%	32.8%	11.2%	7.2%	--%
EBITDA Margin	5.3	4.7	4.0	4.0	4.1	--
Return on Equity	--	--	--	--	--	--
Return on Capital Employed	--	10.7	14.0	15.3	16.7	--
Earnings Per Share — FIL Estimate	--	17.80	21.20	24.60	28.20	--
Earnings Per Share — Street Estimate	--	--	20.22	22.37	--	--
Net Dividend Per Share	--	--	--	--	--	--
Price/Earnings Multiple	--x	12.8x	10.7x	9.2x	8.1x	--
Enterprise Value/EBITDA	--	10.7	8.5	7.5	6.6	--
Enterprise Value/Sales	--	--	--	--	--	--

Sector relative rating. Financial note:

Business Description

Operates licensed betting offices, telephone and online betting operations. Offers odds and takes bets on an assortment of sporting and other events.

Investment Thesis

1) 7%-9% medium term revs growth will be driven by 5%-6% underlying betting revs growth at LBOs + new revs from FOBTs & online betting operations. This translates to 15%+ eps growth.
2) EPS ests 5% ahead of street for 03 and 10% ahead for 04 as I am more bullish on 03 horse betting mgns (10% levy for on course bookies + betting exchanges will lead to higher mgns) + ebit contribution from FOBTs. For 04, I am more bullish on EPOS rollout impact on op mgns.
3) Given growth prospects valuation is attractive with stock trading on 10.9x 03 earnings and 8.5% 03 FCF yield. Stock trades as a defensive but as street catches up with 3 yr growth story, expect eps ests + pe multiple expansion to lead to out performance. Price target = 300p = 14x 03 earnings (32% upside).

HILL(WILLIAM) ORD GBP0.10
3189889
Price relative to MSCI Europe(US$) to Apr. 4, 2003. Jan. 17, 2002 to Apr. 4, 2003
Source: FactSet.

News and Outlook

Strong start to 03: First 9 weeks of year, gross win was up 20% YOY. Growth driven by 8%+ growth in retail underlying betting revs, 20% in internet and revs from hugely popular FOBTs (Fixed odd betting terminals). Slight setback in MArch,with a lot of favourites winning their races at Cheltham. Breakdown of losses for bookies as follows: Ladbrokes £2.2m, William Hill £1.5m, Paddy Power £0.5m (all nos direct from respective companies).

Betting shops: 03 plan is to open up 20 new shops. It has become easier to get new license applications (need to prove there is unsatisfied demand in an area) in advance of gaming deregulation scheduled for summer 04. In addition mgmt is looking to relocate 40 sites. Expect portfolio of shops to be more actively managed going forward as historically there was some incentive to keep poorly performing shops to prevent competitors getting new licenses.

Beyond Paddy Power expanding in the UK (plans to get to 12 shops by 03 end), I do not expect a huge amount of additional competition over the next 3 years. New entrants in my view need to open at least 100 shops, have online + phone operations + spend significant amounts on mktg to have any chance of competing with the existing companies in the industry.

For 03, I expect gross win to be up by 5.5% YOY driven by 2% increase in no of shops, 4% increase in stakes per shop and slightly lower mgns. I have gross win mgn dropping 10 bps YOY to 17.7% due to lower football mix YOY (no World Cup) offsetting increase in horse betting mgns due to new levy + duty on betting exchanges. Risk remains on the upside. With costs up 6% due to NI, rent + wage increases, I have LBO ebit going up 2.6% YOY.

Telephone: Excl World Cup positive in H1 02, H2 02 was flat H/H. Growth lower than expected as William Hill + others have put in min bet sizes in place to encourage customers to use online instead as incremental handling costs are 10% of telephone for online. For 03 I expect gross win to be up 5% YOY (vs. 5.9% growth seen in 02) and ebit to be up 9.2% YOY (increased avg bet size leading to lower cost growth).

Online: H2 02 growth lower than expected due to hit from Hong Kong government making it more difficult for punters to use credit cards on overseas online gaming sites. In 02, 10% of revs came from Hong Kong. Expect a further negative impact in 03.

Big positives for 03 will be
- Higher gross mgn: Across all online sites gross mgns have been going up due to mix of bets in favour of football + weaker startups closing down.
- Growth in casino games gross win: After talking to a no of companies it is now evident that is there is a huge amount of cross over from punters betting on sports/racing to playing casino games.
- Op leverage kicking in: Op leverage now kicking in given incremental processing costs extremely low– in 02 William Hill's internet ebit mgn went up from 3.4% to 5.3%.

For 03, I expect internet gross win to be up 10.5% YOY to £60.6m and ebit to be up 16.5% YOY to £23.9m. Mgmt looking for 20%+ growth in gross win in 03. For now I remain cautious due to potential further negative impact from Hong Kong. Risk to my ests remains on the upside especially if new poker game introduced in Q1 takes off.

FOBTs: Contributed £8m of gross win + £4m of ebit in H2 02. Currently doing £220 of ebit per week per machine. 1820 machines rolled out as at Dec 03 going up to 2000 by March 03. Working thru nos, implies terminals can do £22m+ of ebit per year. In my ests for now I have factored in £17.5m of ebit (20% below 03 potential) as I am slightly cautious re ebit dropping as novelty wears off. However initial anecdotal evidence from talking to punters points to terminal popularity growing as punters start getting used to them.

Update on FOBT test case: Test case will be heard in summer. Gaming Board wants roulette game banned from shops as it is a casino game vs. betting shops arguing it is just another fixed odds game with the results determined off site. Stanley Leisure which has both casinos + betting shops is supporting the betting shops. Once case is decided it will be appealed and hence no final decision likely till summer 04.

Key new development has been the Department of Media & Culture Services (DCMS) view re these machines. Met officials from DCMS looking at FOBTs last week. DCMS view is that test case will not be settled before summer 04 by which time it will be irrelevant as FOBTs will be part of gaming deregulation scheduled for summer 04. FOBTs will be considered to be gaming machines – restrictions as per deregulation proposals are max of 4 machines allowed per shop with max of £500 in prize money. Roulette game is not an issue. If this is the case this will be a big positive for the betting shops

---

Betting exchanges: From 1st of April BetFair now has to pay a 10% levy on the full value of bets made by punters thru BetFair vs. the 10% paid on only its 3% commission on bets. Also on course bokies now have to pay a 10% levy. In addition upcoming budget, indications from a no of sources are that the governement is looking to introduce a 15% gross profit tax on bets going thru betting exchanges. This will put Betfair on a level playing field with off course bookies. Net impact of the above will be at least a 10% step up in horse betting mgns for the off course bookies. More importantly levy + duty will destroys Betfair's business model. Moving offshore to avoid the 15% gross profit duty will help to offset some of the damage but this is not enough in my view.

EPOS roll out: Mgmt guiding to initial tests in Q4 03 before roll out in 04 and 05. Given hugely positive experience on revs to ebit conversion (up from 26% to 51%) seen from EPOS roll out at Ladbrokes in H2 02, William Hill could bring the roll out forward. For now capex breakdown on current rollout as follows: £7m in 03, £14m in 04, £14m in 05 –total £35m
Pension deficit: Liabilities of £130m, assets of £90m – £40m deficit. Assets split: 95% equities and 5% bonds. Due to deficit staff costs going up by £1m per annum from 03.

Valuation/Opinion

Following 02 results + meetings with mgmt, 03 eps est raised by 1% to 21.2p and 04 est up by 3% to 24.6p. Given growth prospects valuation is attractive with stock trading on 10.9x 03 earnings and 8.5% 03 FCF yield. Stock trades as a defensive but as street catches up with 3 yr growth story, expect eps ests + pe multiple expansion to lead to out performance. Price target is 300p = 14x 03 earnings (32% upside).
Risk: CVC and Cinven hold 18% of the shares and are now free to sell their stakes (lock up ended with the publishing of 02 results). Given partners from both are close to business, they are unlikely to sell their stakes for now before expected positive benefits from FOBTs, etc. are reflected in stock price. Not a risk for now but one to watch out for towards end 03.

William Hill

Price (p)	216.5	FCF yield	7.0%
Shares	428.8	Div yield	4.0%
Market cap (£m)	928.4	**Rating**	**2**
EV	1432		

Year to 31 December	1999	% ch	2000	% ch	01 H1A	01 H2A	2001	% ch
LBOs (Licenced Betting Offices)								
Number of shops (period end)							1537	
Number of shops (average)							1537	
Slippage (m)	235		227	-3%			249	9%
Stake/slip	6.22		6.44	4%			6.81	6%
Turnover	**1461**		**1463**	0%	**758.0**	**935.0**	**1693**	16%
Gross win	**337.3**		**352.2**	4%	**195.7**	**187.6**	**383.3**	9%
Gross win percentage	23.1%		24.1%		25.8%	20.1%	22.6%	
Levy	-15.3		-16.3	6.5%	-8.4	-11.0	-19.4	19.0%
Gross profits tax (previously revenue)	-98.7		-98.8	0.1%	-50.9	-43.7	-94.6	-4.3%
Gross contribution after levys	**223.3**		**237.1**	6.2%	**136.4**	**132.9**	**269.3**	13.6%
One benefits - World Cup								
One off costs (pensions, pictures etc)								
Direct staff costs	-79.5		-82.5	3.8%			-91.8	11.3%
Other direct costs	-89.3		-91	1.9%			-103.9	14.2%
Total costs	-168.8		-173.5	2.8%	-93.1	-102.0	-195.1	12.4%
Net trading profit	**54.5**		**63.6**	16.7%	**43.3**	**30.9**	**74.2**	16.7%
AWPs								
Installed machines	2773		2879	3.8%			2969	3.1%
Cash in box/week/machine	212.0		213.0	0.5%			213.0	0.0%
Turnover (gross win less VAT)					13.7	14.7	28.4	
Total cash in box inc VAT (gross win)	**30.6**		**31.9**	4.3%	**16.1**	**17.3**	**33.4**	4.7%
Machine duty	-1.7		-1.8	5.9%			-2.0	11.1%
VAT	-4.6		-4.7	4.3%			-5.0	5.1%
Total machine duty / VAT	-6.3		-6.5	4.7%	-3.4	-3.6	-7.0	
Reported turnover and contribution	**24.3**		**25.3**	4.2%	**12.7**	**13.7**	**26.4**	4.2%
Net trading profit	**17.6**		**19.0**	8.1%	**9.4**	**10.1**	**19.5**	2.5%
FOBTs - incremental EBIT								
Total shop trading profit (LBO & AWP)					**52.7**	**40.5**	**93.2**	
Internet								
Sportsbook								
Active accounts (period end)							100000	
Average no. active accounts	6800		71000				97500	37.3%
Slips/customer/annum	42		60	42.9%			97	61.7%
Stake/slip	35.7		29.8	-16.4%			27.6	-7.5%
Turnover	**10.2**		**127.1**				**260.8**	105.3%
Gross win/customer/annum	89		143	60.7%			232	62.2%
Derived gross win	**0.6**		**10.2**				**22.6**	122.8%
Gross win percentage	5.9%		8.0%				8.7%	
GBD/GPT	-0.1		-2.6		-1.1	-1.6	-2.7	3.8%
Levy	0.0		-0.2		-0.1	-0.5	-0.6	200.0%
Contribution	**0.5**		**7.4**				**19.3**	162.7%
Net trading profit	**-2.9**		**-8.7**				**4.5**	
Casino								
Average no. active accounts			18700				35600	90.4%
Gross win/customer/annum			324				351	8.3%
Derived gross win			**6.1**				**12.5**	106.2%
Net trading profit			**1.0**				**4.7**	389.7%
Total Internet								
Turnover	**10.2**		**133.1**		**111.3**	**162.0**	**273.3**	
Gross Win	**0.6**		**16.2**		**14.0**	**21.1**	**35.1**	
- gross win %					12.6%	13.0%	12.8%	
Trading profit	**-2.9**		**-7.8**		**2.5**	**6.7**	**9.2**	
- trading profit %					2.2%	4.1%	3.4%	
Telephone								
Average no. active accounts	167000		188000	12.6%			151000	-19.7%
Slips/customer/annum	30		29	-2.7%			44	51.4%
Stake/slip	56.47		61.86	9.5%			62.91	1.7%
Turnover	**283**		**340**	20.0%	**179.3**	**240.6**	**419.9**	23.6%
Gross win/customer/annum	264		254	-3.8%			318	25.2%
Derived gross win	**44.1**		**47.7**	8.3%	**24.9**	**23.1**	**48.0**	0.6%
Gross win percentage	15.6%		14.1%		13.9%	9.6%	11.4%	
Levy	-2.7		-1.5	-43.0%	-0.5	-1.2	-1.7	10.4%
GBD/GPT	-19.1		-10.7	-43.8%	-3.7	-3.5	-7.2	-33.0%
Contribution	**22.3**		**35.5**	59.1%	**20.7**	**18.4**	**39.1**	10.3%
Net trading profit	**10.1**		**16.4**	62.1%	**7.6**	**8.0**	**15.6**	-4.5%

02 H1A	% ch	02 H1E	% ch	2002E	% ch	2003E	% ch	2004E	% ch	2005E	% ch	2006E	% ch	2007E	% ch
				1575		1583		1583		1583		1583		1583	
				1556	1.2%	1579	1.5%	1583	0.3%	1583	0.0%	1583	0.0%	1583	0.0%
				303	22%	317	3.0%	327	3.0%	337	3.0%	347	3.0%	358	3.0%
				7.5	10%	7.6	1.0%	7.6	1.0%	7.7	1.0%	7.8	1.0%	7.9	1.0%
1124	48%	1148	23%	2272	34%	2398	5.6%	2501	4.3%	2602	4.0%	2707	4.0%	2816	4.0%
198.2	1.3%	181.7	-3.2%	379.9	-0.9%	396.9	4.5%	412.8	4.0%	429.3	4.0%	446.5	4.0%	464.4	4.0%
17.6%		15.8%		16.7%		16.5%		16.5%		16.5%		16.5%		16.5%	
-10.6	26.2%	-12.2	10.8%	-22.8	17.5%	-23.8	4.5%	-24.8	4.0%	-25.8	4.0%	-26.8	4.0%	-27.9	4.0%
-29.7	-41.7%	-27.3	-37.6%	-57.0	-39.8%	-59.5	4.5%	-61.9	4.0%	-64.4	4.0%	-67.0	4.0%	-69.7	4.0%
157.9	15.8%	142.2	7.0%	300.1	11.4%	313.6	4.5%	326.1	4.0%	339.2	4.0%	352.7	4.0%	366.9	4.0%
				-5				0		0		0		0	
				-108	18.0%	-115	6.0%	-119	3.5%	-123	3.5%	-127	3.5%	-132	3.5%
				-104	0.1%	-110	6.0%	-115	4.5%	-119	3.5%	-123	3.5%	-128	3.5%
-106.2	14.0%	-111.1	9.0%	-217.3	11.4%	-225.1	3.6%	-234.0	4.0%	-242.2	3.5%	-250.7	3.5%	-259.5	3.5%
51.7	19.4%	31.0	0.4%	82.8	11.5%	88.5	7.0%	92.1	4.0%	96.9	5.3%	102.0	5.2%	107.4	5.2%
				2999	1.0%	3029	0.0%	3059	0.0%	3090	0.0%	3120	0.0%	3152	0.0%
				221.5	6.0%	223.7	-15.0%	217.0	-3.0%	219.2	1.0%	221.4	1.0%	223.6	1.0%
14.9	8.8%	15.5	5.7%	30.4	7.2%	25.9	-15.0%	25.1	-3.0%	25.3	1.0%	25.6	1.0%	25.9	1.0%
17.5	8.7%	18.3	5.5%	35.8	7.1%	30.4	-15.0%	29.5	-3.0%	29.8	1.0%	30.1	1.0%	30.4	1.0%
				-2.0	2.0%	-2.1	5.0%	-2.2	1.0%	-2.2	1.0%	-2.2	1.0%	-2.2	1.0%
				-5.3	6.7%	-4.5	-15.0%	-4.4	-3.0%	-4.4	1.0%	-4.5	1.0%	-4.5	1.0%
-3.6	5.9%	-3.8	4.8%	-7.4	5.3%	-6.7		-6.6		-6.6		-6.7		-6.8	
13.9	9.4%	14.5	5.7%	28.4	7.5%	23.7	-16.4%	22.9	-3.4%	23.2	1.0%	23.4	1.0%	23.6	1.0%
10.4	10.4%	10.6	5.3%	21.0	7.8%	16.0	-24.0%	14.8	-7.4%	14.6	-1.2%	14.4	-1.3%	14.2	-1.5%
		1.0		1.0		8.0		10.4	30%	11.4	10%	12.6	10%	13.8	10%
62.1	17.8%	42.7	5.4%	104.8	12.4%	112.5	7.4%	117.3	4.2%	123.0	4.9%	129.0	4.9%	135.4	4.9%
126000				134550	38.0%	150696	12.0%	168780	12.0%	185657	10.0%	200510	8.0%	212541	6.0%
				112		117	5.0%	121	3.0%	124	3.0%	128	3.0%	132	3.0%
				29.2	6.0%	29.2	0.0%	29.2	0.0%	29.2	0.0%	29.2	0.0%	29.2	0.0%
				438.8	68.2%	516.0	17.6%	595.3	15.4%	674.4	13.3%	750.3	11.2%	819	9.2%
				313.2	35.0%	322.6	3.0%	332.3	3.0%	342.2	3.0%	352.5	3.0%	363.1	3.0%
				42.1	86.3%	48.6	15.4%	56.1	15.4%	63.5	13.3%	70.7	11.2%	77.2	9.2%
				9.6%		9.4%		9.4%		9.4%		9.4%		9.4%	
-3.1		-3.2		-6.3	134.1%	-7.3	15.4%	-8.4	15.4%	-9.5	13.3%	-10.6	11.2%	-11.6	9.2%
-0.7		-1.2		-1.9	216.1%	-1.6	-15.4%	-1.9	-15.4%	-2.1	13.3%	-2.3	11.2%	-2.5	9.2%
				33.9	75.6%	39.7	17.1%	45.8	15.4%	51.9	13.3%	57.7	11.2%	63.0	9.2%
				17.2	280.8%	21.9	27.3%	27.1	23.8%	32.3	19.0%	37.1	15.0%	41.4	11.5%
				49840	40.0%	55821	12.0%	61403	10.0%	64473	5.0%	67697	5.0%	71082	5.0%
				379	8.0%	387	2.0%	394	2.0%	402	2.0%	410	2.0%	419	2.0%
				18.9	51.2%	21.6	14.2%	24.2	12.2%	25.9	7.1%	27.8	7.1%	29.8	7.1%
				8.2	73.8%	9.2	13.3%	10.7	15.4%	11.5	7.6%	12.3	7.5%	13.3	7.5%
197.6	78%	260.1	61%	457.7	67.4%	537.6	17.5%	619.5	15.2%	700.4	13.1%	778.0	11.1%	849	9.1%
29.3	109%	31.7	50%	61.0	73.8%	70.2	15.0%	80.3	14.4%	89.5	11.4%	98.5	10.0%	106.9	8.6%
14.8%		12.2%		13.3%		13.1%		13.0%		12.8%		12.7%		12.6%	
11.3	352%	14.1	110%	25.4	175.3%	31.2	22.8%	37.8	21.3%	43.8	15.8%	49.5	13.1%	54.7	10.5%
5.7%		5.4%		5.5%		5.8%		6.1%		6.2%		6.4%		6.4%	
				160060	6.0%	163261	2.0%	166526	2.0%	169857	2.0%	173254	2.0%	176719	2.0%
				45	1.0%	45	1.0%	46	1.0%	46	1.0%	46	1.0%	47	1.0%
				64.80	3.0%	66.09	2.0%	67.42	2.0%	68.76	2.0%	70.14	2.0%	71.54	2.0%
243.5	36%	219.5	-9%	463.0	10.3%	486.5	5.1%	511.2	5.1%	537.2	5.1%	564.5	5.1%	593	5.1%
				324.4	2.0%	330.8	2.0%	337.5	2.0%	344.2	2.0%	351.1	2.0%	358.1	2.0%
27.5	10%	24.4	6%	51.9	8.1%	54.0	4.0%	56.2	4.0%	58.5	4.0%	60.8	4.0%	63.3	4.0%
11.3%		11.1%		11.2%		11.1%		11.0%		10.9%		10.8%		10.7%	
-1.9	280%	-1.7	45%	-3.6	113.8%	-3.8	4.0%	-3.9	4.0%	-4.1	4.0%	-4.3	4.0%	-4.4	4.0%
-4.2	14%	-3.6	3%	-7.8	8.2%	-8.1	4.0%	-8.4	4.0%	-8.8	4.0%	-9.1	4.0%	-9.5	4.0%
21.4	3%	19.1	4%	40.5	3.5%	42.1	4.0%	43.8	4.0%	45.6	4.0%	47.4	4.0%	49.4	4.0%
9.1	20%	7.9	-1%	17.0	9.1%	18.0	5.5%	18.9	5.4%	20.0	5.4%	21.0	5.4%	22.2	5.3%

William Hill		Price (p)		216.5	FCF yield	7.0%		
		Shares		428.8	Div yield	4.0%		
		Market cap (£m)		928.4	**Rating**	2		
		EV		1432				

Year to 31 December	1999	% ch	2000	% ch	01 H1A	01 H2A	2001	% ch
Other								
Turnover (on track, Isle of Man, index bets)	97.5		78.7		24.1	13.3	37.4	
Gross profit	4.2		4.0		1.5	1.0	2.5	
Other trading profit	-0.5		-1.3		-0.5	-0.2	-0.7	
Central costs	-8.3		-10.6	27.7%	-4.4	-5.8	-10.2	-3.8%
Net trading profit	**-8.8**		**-11.9**	35.2%	**-4.9**	**-6.0**	**-10.9**	-8.4%
P&L								
Total turnover	1,878		2,042	8.8%	1,086	1,366	2,452	20.1%
Divisional Gross profit	417		452	8.5%	252.2	250	502.6	11.2%
- Gross profit margin	22.2%		22.1%		23.2%	18.3%	20.5%	
Trading profit (pre-exceps)	70.5		79.0	12.0%	57.9	49.7	107.6	36.2%
- trading margin	3.8%		3.9%		5.3%	3.6%	4.4%	
Share of SIS/other non-trading	5.2		5.6		2.6	2.3	4.9	
Exceptionals/goodwill	-26.5							
EBIT (pre-exceps)	**49.2**		**84.6**	71.9%	**60.5**	**52.0**	**112.5**	33.0%
Interest	-108.3		-81.6		43.0	-127.7	-84.7	
PBT	**-59.1**		**3.0**				**27.8**	827.0%
Tax	2.9		-2.1				-8.9	
Tax rate	5%		70%				32%	
Net profit	**-56.2**		**0.9**				**18.9**	
Dividends paid	0.0		0.0				0.0	
Retained profit	-56.2		0.9				18.9	
Shares outstanding	428.8		428.8				428.8	
EPS	**-0.13**		**0.00**				**0.04**	
DPS	0.00		0.00				0.00	
DPS cover								
Cashflow								
EBIT	74		85		57.9		112	
Depreciation	11.8		14.0		8.9		16.6	
Working capital	3.4		8.0		13.3		9.5	
Associate income	-3.9		-5.6				-4.9	
Other	0		0		1.5		0	
Net cashflow from operating activities	**86**		**101**		**81.6**		**133**	
Net interest paid	n.a		n.a				n.a	
Dividends from associates	n.a		n.a				n.a	
Dividends paid to plc shareholders	n.a		n.a				n.a	
Net cash outflow from investment / finance	**n.a**		**n.a**				**n.a**	
Tax paid (net)	**n.a**		**n.a**				**n.a**	
Net cash inflow before investing activities	**n.a**		**n.a**				**n.a**	
Investing activities								
Net capital expenditure	-17.8		-20.2				-20.0	
Acquisitions	n.a		n.a				n.a	
Net cash outflow from investing activities								
FCF								
Net cash inflow/(outflow) before financing								
Other								
Opening Debt								
Closing Debt								
Average debt								
Shareholder funds								
Ratios								
P/E			1027.4				49.0	
EV								
EBITDA			99				129	
EBITDA margin			4.8%				5.3%	
EV/EBITDA								
EV/EBIT								
EV/Sales								
FCF yield								
Div yield								
ROCE - EBIT less tax								

02 H1A	% ch	02 H1E	% ch	2002E	% ch	2003E	% ch	2004E	% ch	2005E	% ch	2006E	% ch	2007E	% ch
12.4	-49%	17.6	32%	30.0		35.0		35.0		35.0		35.0		35.0	
1.2	-20%	2.0	100%	3.2		3.9		3.9		3.9		3.9		3.9	
0.3		0.0		0.3		0.3		0.3		0.3		0.3		0.3	
-4.5		-4.5		-9.0	5.0%	-9.9	10.0%	-10.4	5.0%	-10.9	5.0%	-11.5	5.0%	-12.0	5.0%
-4.2		-4.5		-8.7	-20.2%	-9.6	10.3%	-10.1	5.2%	-10.6	5.1%	-11.2	5.1%	-11.7	5.1%
1,593	46.6%	1,660	21.6%	3,253	32.7%	3,483	7.1%	3,692	6.0%	3,900	5.6%	4,110	5.4%	4,319	5.1%
273.7	8.5%	226	-9.6%	532	5.8%	555	4.5%	583	4.9%	611	4.8%	640	4.7%	669	4.5%
17.2%		13.6%		16.3%		15.9%		15.8%		15.7%		15.6%		15.5%	
78.3		60.2		138.5	28.7%	152.0	9.8%	163.9	7.8%	176.1	7.4%	188.4	7.0%	200.5	6.4%
4.9%		3.6%		4.3%		4.4%		4.4%		4.5%		4.6%		4.6%	
1.8		1.1		2.9		2.2		2.2		2.2		2.2		2.2	
-20.1		0.0		-20.1											
80.1		61.3		141.4	25.6%	154.2	9.1%	166.1	7.7%	178.3	7.3%	190.6	6.9%	202.7	6.4%
-17.5		-17.5		-35.0		-30.1		-27.3		-23.8		-18.9		-15.0	
				106.4	282.1%	124.1	16.7%	138.8	11.8%	154.5	11.3%	171.7	11.1%	187.7	9.3%
				-30.9		-36.0		-40.3		-44.8		-49.8		-54.4	
				29%		29%		29%		29%		29%		29%	
				75.5	298.8%	88.1	16.7%	98.6	11.8%	109.7	11.3%	121.9	11.1%	133.3	9.3%
				-37.3		-43.5		-48.7		-54.2		-60.2		-65.8	
				38.2		44.6		49.9		55.5		61.7		67.5	
				428.8		428.8		428.8		428.8		428.8		428.8	
				0.176	298.8%	0.206	16.7%	0.230	11.8%	0.256	11.3%	0.284	11.1%	0.311	9.3%
				0.09		0.10		0.11		0.13		0.14		0.15	
				0.49		0.49		0.49		0.49		0.49		0.49	
58.2				141		154		166		178		191		203	
7.9				18.3		21.9		26.3		28.9		31.8		35.0	
9.9				10.0		0.0		0.0		0.0		0.0		0.0	
				0.0		0.0		0.0		0.0		0.0		0.0	
2.6				2.6		0		0		0		0		0	
78.6				172.3		176.2		192.4		207.2		222.4		237.7	
-30.9				-35		-30		-27		-24		-19		-15	
0				0		0		0		0		0		0	
0				-37		-44		-49		-54		-60		-66	
-30.9				-72		-74		-76		-78		-79		-81	
-3.2				-3		-36.0		-40.3		-44.8		-49.8		-54.4	
44.5				97		67		76		84		94		102	
-10.3				-25		-45		-45		-25		-25		-25	
				-21		0		0		0		0		0	
				-46		-45		-45		-25		-25		-25	
				109.1		65.1		79.9		113.6		128.7		143.3	
34.2				50.7		21.5		31.2		59.5		68.5		77.5	
288.0															
-792				-520		-453		-432		-401		-341		-273	
-470				-453		-432		-401		-341		-273		-195	
-631				-503		-443		-416		-371		-307		-234	
				254		298		348		404		466		533	
				12.3		10.5		9.4		8.5		7.6		7.0	
				1432		1371		1345		1299		1235		1162	
				160		176		192		207		222		238	
				4.9%		5.1%		5.2%		5.3%		5.4%		5.5%	
				9.0		7.8		7.0		6.3		5.6		4.9	
				10.1		8.9		8.1		7.3		6.5		5.7	
				0.44		0.39		0.36		0.33		0.30		0.27	
				11.7%		7.0%		8.6%		12.2%		13.9%		15.4%	
				4.0%		4.7%		5.2%		5.8%		6.5%		7.1%	
				13.3%		14.8%		15.4%		16.3%		17.5%		18.8%	

7. Pages of the first managers report: October 1980

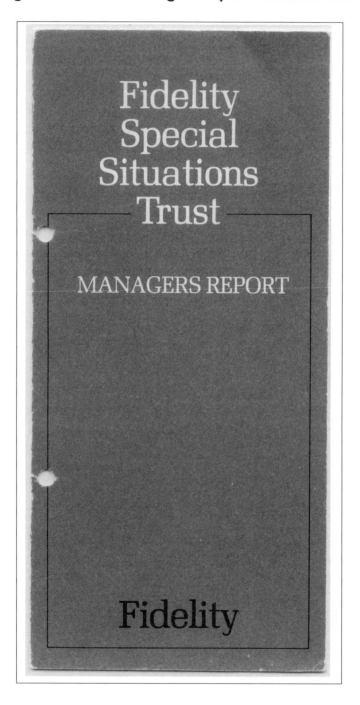

MANAGERS REPORT

Since the launch of the Trust some 9 months ago in December 1979 the offer price of the units has risen 54.4%, from 25.0p to 38.6p at 1st October 1980. During the same period the F. T. Actuaries All-Share Index has risen 23.6%. As these figures suggest the U.K. Stock Market has been firm during this period and, after some consolidation in March, April and May, the All-Share Index has recently risen into all time high ground. The 30 Share Index has lagged behind (up 11.6%) mainly reflecting the relative weakness of the shares of many leading manufacturing companies.

It has been an excellent environment for Special Situation Companies. Notable successes have been the following:

Company	Net Profit	Average Holding Period
C. T. Bowring 10% conv.	26%	4 months
Candecca	95%	5 months
Elsburg Gold	61%	1 month
Gough Cooper	33%	2 months
Howard Johnson	40%	1 month
Tebbitt Group	43%	1 week
Ultramar	20%	1 month
KCA	20%	4 months
Geers Gross	19%	6 months

Unlike profits made by individual investors these realised profits within the Trust are completely free of capital gains tax as a result of the change of rules in the last Budget. Thus 100% of these profits were reinvested in other attractive situations as against only 70% if they had been made by private investors liable to capital gains tax. Over 60% of the current portfolio are shares purchased in the last two months highlighting the managers active policy. Good prof. on shares still retained are: First National Finance Corp up 34%, Strata Oil up 84%, London Investment Trust up 33% and Carliol Investment Trust up over 60%. Of course there have been some disappointments as will always happen with a Trust of this nature: the settlement terms for the Rhodesian Bonds were below market expectations and our holding was cut at a loss.

The investment policy of the Trust is described in greater detail in the next section. Given the mixed outlook for many companies at the current time and the increased volatility of the market as a whole, we believe that full-time active professional management and the policy followed by this Trust are more relevant today than ever and should continue to produce above average results. Additionally, we believe that trends have already started within the economy and the financial environment which could make the eighties a very much more attractive period than the seventies for equity investments in general.

1st October 1980

Anthony Bolton
Richard Timberlake

Aim of the Trust

The aim of this Trust is to produce above average capital appreciation from a diversified portfolio of undervalued 'Special Situations'.

What is a Special Situation?

Almost any share at a particular time can be a special situation. In general it will be a company attractively valued in relation to net assets, dividend yield or future earnings per share, but additionally having some other specific attraction that could have a positive short term influence on the share price. Often the price action in these situations will show above average volatility resulting in higher risk as well as higher potential reward. Special Situations tend to fall into the following categories: small growth stocks, recovery shares, asset situations, new issues, companies involved in bids, energy and resource stocks, companies reorganising or changing their business and new technology situations. Authorised Unit Trusts are allowed to invest up to 5% of their assets in unquoted securities and from time to time use is made of this concession.

Sources of Ideas

A wide range of ideas for potential holdings in the Trust is sought from over fifty London and Regional Stockbrokers with whom Fidelity is in close contact. With small local companies the Regional Stockbroker's help is invaluable. Other sources are Fidelity's own research capabilities both in the U.K. and overseas. Regular contact is maintained with Fidelity's large Research Department in Boston and the Fidelity investment managers based in America and around the world involved in the management of Fidelity's International Funds.

The Portfolio

These large numbers of ideas are then sifted by the investment manager to arrive at a concentrated portfolio of about 30-40 shares from several of the categories mentioned above, each new idea being judged against the current portfolio. By holding a portfolio of 30 or more shares the volatility and risk inherent in any individual share is greatly diminished. The holdings are continually monitored and re-assessed, and are sold either when they have achieved their objective or when a better idea is found.

As a result the management of the portfolio tends to be fairly active and the turnover is high. Shares that fail to live up to expectations are sold (even if this is at a loss) to reduce the "opportunity cost" of missing a better situation. Short term profits are often taken and this general policy of active management has been made more attractive by the recent change in the law ending the liability to any capital gains tax within authorised Unit Trusts.

The flexibility is also retained to invest a proportion of the Fund overseas, although this proportion is usually not more than 20% of the Trust. Overseas shares are chosen on a similar basis to U.K. shares. As well as increasing substantially the investment opportunities this overseas diversification has the advantage of further reducing the overall volatility of the portfolio.

The Trust is usually fully invested and market timing decisions are not normally attempted.

The Dividend Policy

Because the Trust aims to have maximum flexibility to seek out the best opportunities for capital gain the income yield may vary considerably from year to year and the managers are not restricted by the requirement to pay a dividend at least as high as the previous year.

Income

The distribution for Special Situations units payable on 15th October 1980 amounts to 0.43p net per unit.

An Attractive Strategy

Nearly always, whatever the overall stock market trend, Special Situations exist. The Trust's fully invested policy forces the manager to seek out such shares and to identify the most attractive.

APPLICATION FORM

To: **Fidelity International Management Limited**
Buckingham House, 62/63 Queen St.,
London EC4R 1AD

Registered Office as above. Registered in England No. 1448245.

I/We wish to invest £ _____
in units of Fidelity Special Situations Trust
at the offer price ruling on receipt of this application.
I/We enclose a remittance payable to 'Fidelity International Management Limited'.

Minimum initial investment is £500

Tick boxes for the following:

Automatic re-investment of income ☐
Details of the Share Exchange Scheme ☐
Details of Fidelity Gilt and Fixed Interest Trust ☐
Fidelity Maximum Income Equity Trust ☐
Fidelity Growth + Income Trust ☐
Fidelity American Trust ☐
Fidelity American Special Situation Trust ☐

Surname _____
(Mr/Mrs/Miss)
First name(s) in full_____
Address _____
_____
_____

Post Code _____
I am/We are over 18 years old.

Signature(s) _____

_____
(if there are joint applicants, all must sign and attach names and addresses separately.)

AGENT'S STAMP

VAT Number

Author's acknowledgements

In producing this book I have benefited enormously from the help and advice of many investment professionals, both within and outside Fidelity. Apart from Anthony Bolton, those inside the company who have either talked to me or provided invaluable assistance include: Barry Bateman, Simon Fraser, Sally Walden, Graham Clapp, Bill Byrnes, Rick Spillane, Caroline King, Matthew White, Paul Kafka (now at the London Stock Exchange), Joerg Moberg and Richard Miles. Outside Fidelity I have drawn on the insights and experience of: Richard Timberlake, Peter Jeffreys, Alex Hammond-Chambers, Edward Bonham Carter, Ian Rushbrook, John Chatfeild-Roberts, Sir Charles Fraser, John Kay, Nils Taube, Crispin Odey, Mark Tyndall, David Fuller, Barry Riley, Elroy Dimson, Peter Hargreaves, Charlie Ellis, Ken Fisher and Mark Dampier. I am grateful to Alastair MacDougall, Head of Research at WM Company, and Lee Gardhouse, Fund of funds manager at Hargreaves Lansdown, for providing professional assessments of the performance of Fidelity Special Situations (included as appendices), and to Standard & Poor's, Caspian Publishing and Close Winterflood Securities for permission to reproduce material. Special thanks are due to Philip Jenks, Myles Hunt and Nick Read of Harriman House for committing themselves so enthusiastically to this project, the first I hope of many similar collaborations. Finally I am grateful to Kristin van Santen and my two children, Nick and Anna Davis, for providing their own unique and valued brand of support during the production of this book.

Bath and London
November 2004